STAFF AND EDUCATIONAL DEVELOPMENT ASSOCIATION

Never Mind the Teaching Feel the Learning

by

Professor Phil Race

University of Glamorgan

SEDA Paper 80
June 1993
Reprinted November 1994
ISBN 0 946815 53 4

Never mind the teaching - feel the learning

Phil Race

Introduction

This is an anthology of workshop papers, conference papers and workshop reports on a mixture of themes, including assessment, open learning, appraisal and large classes. The common thread is learner-centredness. The title of the anthology is taken from the most recent part of the collection - a heartfelt plea to build discussion of the quality of the learning experience into systems for measuring quality in education and training. There are 11 chapters in all, and in most of them I have included an 'Abstract' at the start, which I hope will help busy colleagues to decide which of them they may wish to explore in more depth.

Chapter 1: 'How Real People Learn' introduces my own model of learning which is referred to in many of the subsequent chapters. My claim for this model is that it is down-to-earth and realistic, and more easily lends itself as a focus for designing improvements to teaching and learning processes than is possible with some of the more obscure models of learning. Sometimes people have called my model 'the Anglo-Saxon one' to distinguish it from other models describing the same things, but in long words with Latin roots! Chapter 2 'Never Mind the Teaching - Feel the Learning' builds further on this model, this time in search of quality indicators for learning. Chapter 3: 'Developing Competence' is in a way yet another model of learning, this time concentrating on ways of describing and clarifying learning outcomes.

Chapter 4: 'Quality in Assessment' is the first in four provocative pieces about assessment, most of which criticise the reliance that has been placed on traditional forms of assessment such as written exams. Chapter 5: 'BS 5750 for Assessment' is not really about BS 5750, but it is about criteria for quality in assessment processes and instruments. Chapter 6: 'Getting the Assessment Right' sums up my concerns about traditional approaches to assessment, this time in the language of a magazine article which caused quite a stir! The final chapter of the assessment section is Chapter 7: 'Appraising Assessment'. I developed this from the report I made of a workshop about assessment at a conference about appraisal.

The next two chapters are about open and flexible learning - an area that I have worked in quite a lot over the last decade. Chapter 8: 'Designing for Open Learning' is a short piece intended to whet people's appetites regarding experimenting in 'packaging-up' parts of their teaching into flexible learning formats. Chapter 9 'Towards Flexible Learning Quality' is a more extended analysis of the main features of flexible learning, including a list of criteria for high quality in resource materials.

The final two chapters deal with somewhat separate issues, yet ones which most teachers in higher and further education face now. Chapter 10: 'Need More Mean Worse?' looks at the dangers of trying to work with larger numbers of learners, but also at the opportunities this presents. The volume ends with Chapter 11: 'Help Yourself to Appraisal?' This is intended to be useful to appraisees rather than appraisers.

There are various ways that this anthology may be used including as a dip-in resource, or a reader for a staff development programme. I've tried to avoid jargon and to put my ideas across in a direct informal way. However, my strongest hope is that individual colleagues in higher and further education will simply find that it is a useful source of ideas they can experiment with and develop further and that they will feel that the volume is a friend and not a threat.

Phil Race, May 1993

Contents

Chapter 1

How real people learn
- not what educational psychologists think!

Abstract

There is no divide between education and training when we look at the purposes of both - to engender **learning**. The intentions of all trainers, teachers, educators, tutors, workshop facilitators, learning-resource designers, and textbook authors converge: to make learning possible.

There is naturally a vast literature on the subject of how people learn. After all, there is documentary evidence that human beings have been learning for some thousands of years. Surprisingly, much of the literature about learning has only been written during this century, and (even more surprisingly) most of it has been written by psychologists. While there is no doubt that psychologists themselves have learned a great deal, perhaps they are not always quite in tune with how the rest of the species actually learns.

This interactive chapter aims to involve readers in addressing two personal questions about their own achievements and the processes whereby they made these achievements. Additionally, they will be asked to address the cause of any *unsuccessful* learning experience they may have had (if they dare admit to having had such a thing!).

From typical responses to these questions, a simple 'theory' of learning is drawn. I claim that this 'theory' of learning has the practical advantage that it enables teachers, tutors, educators, workshop facilitators, trainers - and everyone else whose job includes helping people to learn - to build their work around the ways that people really learn, and (even more importantly) it provides a useful model which allows learners themselves to find out a great deal about how they themselves can make their learning more effective, more efficient, and more enjoyable.

Many of the remaining chapters in this book are linked to the model of learning proposed in the present chapter.

The need to focus on learning

Whatever sort of training we think about, or whatever sort of educational experience we consider, the one thing they all need to have in common is 'learning'. The human species is unique in its capacity for learning - that is why the species has evolved as much as it has. Human beings have learned ever since the dawn of civilisation (and for quite some time before either of the words 'education' or 'training' were invented). Yet much that has been written about *how* we learn tends to have used language which is closer to the ways that educational psychologists think, than to the ways in which the vast majority of human beings learn. In this chapter, I would like to lead readers through their own answers to three basic questions about learning and to propose a simple yet powerful model of learning. I further propose that this model of learning can be of direct use to trainers and educators in ways which have eluded some of the more complex models of learning.

Question 1: about successful learning and demonstrable competence

Getting people to think of something they have learned successfully is a positive start to alerting them to the ways in which they learn. It does not matter what they think of as the successful learning experience of their choice - it can be work-related, or a sporting achievement, or any practical or intellectual skill. Try it for yourself - complete the exercise below before reading on.

Think of something you're good at - something you know you do well.

Write down a few words explaining *how* you became good at it.

It does not seem to matter at all what people choose for the thing they're good at. It also does not seem to matter what sort of people they are. On the next couple of pages, I've transcribed responses I gathered from some very different groups.

The professional view?
Here is a collection of responses to the second part of the above exercise I obtained recently from a distinguished group of people from education, training and publishing.

- Playing/practising/having some coaching.
- Practising - reflecting on it - talking to others and reflecting again.
- Trial and error, reading, observing, experimenting, remembering what worked.
- Reading, discussion, practice, reflection on practice/post-mortem!
- By doing it, by thinking about how to do it better, by talking to people about it, by getting feedback on how well I did it.
- Don't know - teasing out maths problems?
- Years of action research with learners of all ages; observation, reflection on data, trying again, developing method and theory.
- Did it, saw whether/how it worked, reflected on why, tried again.
- Practice, trying different methods.

How real people learn

- Observation - how others did it; aspiration - where I wanted to get to; practice - reflect on mistakes.
- By practice, by concentrating to the exclusion of other things.
- By doing it not so well a lot and thinking about it.

The learners' view?

I posed the same question to a large group of students, this time getting them to write down not only how they became good at things, but also what exactly they claimed to be good at. Not surprisingly, the answers included some which make one smile.

driving	lessons, test, practice
playing the piano	practice, lessons
sex	practice, pleasure, pain
dancing	practice, lessons, experience
gardening	experience, reading about it, talking and listening to gardeners
painting	taught techniques, then practice and experimentation
essays	practice
table tennis	taught, practice, time, experience, sticking with it, endeavour
cooking	practice, necessity, interest
acting	practice, taught techniques by tutor, involving myself in pantomimes
driving	taking lessons, passing a test, driving daily, continuing to learn
driving	perseverance, determination, good teaching, patience, bribing examiner!
embroidery	taught basics, practice and own mistakes
painting	practice, natural ability
playing clarinet	practice, making mistakes, help from others, books, threats
swimming	starting young, practice, taking tests
swimming	practice, enjoyment
playing flute	practice, passing exams, tutoring
drinking beer	extended practice, socialising
sex	practice, pain, pleasure and struggle and hard work
tennis	practice, hard work
playing pool	practice, interest, advice, watching others
wallpapering	watching somebody qualified
mix concrete	by trial and error after being shown how to do it
catering for 90	practice (no choice - dropped in at deep end)
making model aircraft	practice
drawing	practice, looking at mistakes, not being afraid to make mistakes, experimenting, analysing mistakes
ballet	practice, lessons, good teacher, enthusiastic at progress
drawing	practice, lessons, encouragement
talking	practice, discussions with other people
sewing	being taught, practice, enjoying doing it so practising more

How real people learn

A further common thread which can be inferred from many of the students' responses above is that there is a strong connection between their developing confidence and developing competence (whatever the variety). To sum up, the most frequent answers to this question are along the following lines:

- practice
- by doing it
- by trial and error
- by getting it wrong at first and learning from mistakes

Relatively few people give answers such as 'by being trained' or 'by being taught' or 'by listening to experts' or 'by reading about it'. So one key to learning is 'doing'. There's nothing new about this - it's already been called 'experiential learning' for long enough - but let's stay with short words like 'doing' for the present.

Question 2: about developing positive feelings

The matter of *feelings* is something which I think has not been sufficiently explored by the developers of theories of learning. Feelings are as much about what it is to be human as any other aspect of humanity. Yet a relatively simple question yields a wealth of information about the connection between feelings and successful learning. Try this for yourself.

> Think of something about yourself that you *feel* good about -
> a personal quality or attribute - something that 'gives you a bit
> of a glow'.
>
> Write down a few words explaining *why* you feel good about it.
> In other words, upon what *evidence* do you base your positive feeling?

My group of distinguished educationalists, trainers and publishers gave the following answers to the second of the questions above.

- Other people's responses.
- Reactions of others - feedback from others
- Fun, I enjoy it, it feels good, it feels right.
- Because I don't feel good about not doing it; because I was told it was a good thing to do.
- Good feedback, seeing results, helping others to achieve things.
- Sense of pleasure, contentment, excitement.
- Other people's reactions.
- Compliments - reinforcement from others
- Quality of finished task - concrete achievement.
- Feedback from others over a long period.
- When I do it, I feel it 'works' - it's easy to do it well. Others confirm this for me.
- People tell me they like it, positive feedback written/spoken.

How real people learn

A group of students gave very similar responses as follows:

- other people tell me so
- feedback
- interaction
- measuring self against others, imparting information to others
- a combination of self assessment and assessment and observation of others
- continual feedback
- feedback, appreciation, self-confidence, recognition
- people have told me
- results, informal feedback

Therefore, by far the most frequent answers are along the following lines:

- reactions of other people
- feedback
- compliments
- seeing the results

All of these amount to 'feedback' of one sort or another. Relatively few people claim that the origin of their positive feelings comes from within. Most people need to have approval from fellow human-beings to develop a really positive feeling about something. Positive feelings are a crucial stepping stone along the way towards successful learning. Indeed, two of the most common things that can prevent successful learning are the absence of positive feedback or the reception of *negative* feedback. Criticism or disapproval can be powerful contributors to unsuccessful learning.

'Doing' + 'Feedback' = successful learning?

Though these two elements are essential ingredients of successful learning, there are two further things that need to be in place. These two things are easier to tease out by asking a question about *unsuccessful learning*. Try it for yourself now, then read on.

Think of something that you *don't* do well - for example, an unsuccessful learning experience.

Write down a few words describing the *causes* of this unsuccessful learning experience - what went wrong?

Here are some answers which the second of these questions yielded:

The causes of some unsuccessful learning experiences we had:

- No chance to practise; sheer lack of ability.
- My inability to fathom technical information; no human help given?
- I never learned how to 'get on the wavelength' of those who do it well.
- I was warned by my father not to become competent at this activity.

How real people learn

- Did not make sense; felt bad. Could not get to grips with it. Social pressure.
- Insufficient commitment by teacher.
- Never knew when I was doing well/badly. Didn't practise sufficiently. Began too late.
- The explanation was given at too rapid a speed without any acknowledgement of need to reflect and digest.
- Failure of confidence. Possibly I didn't really need to do it? Motivation problem?
- Insufficient practice.
- Unrealistic explanations; damning feedback (or none).
- Not allowing enough extra time to make good choices.
- I didn't model it physically, kinaesthetically; I didn't get help with this.

The answers which emerge from these questions are quite complex, but the general trends hardly vary at all between very different groups in terms of age, experience, profession or vocation. It has to be said that a not infrequent response is for people to write down the name of their best-remembered mathematics teacher! However, apart from this, a pattern emerges quite readily. For a start, there are usually some answers which relate to something having gone wrong with the two essentials we've already looked at. For example:

- lack of opportunity to practise, or to learn safely from mistakes;
- 'bad' feedback - critical feedback given in a hostile or negative way.

But looking for further factors, the following are often found in people's answers:

- no motivation
- fear of failure
- couldn't see why it was worth doing
- lack of time to make sense of it
- unable to understand it before moving on.

These boil down to two further essentials for successful learning: **'wanting'** and **'digesting'**. Let's next look at each of these in turn in a little more detail.

'Wanting'
If there's something wrong with one's motivation, it's unlikely that successful learning will happen. However, 'motivation' is a rather 'cold' word - a psychologists' word rather than everyone's word. 'Wanting' is a much more 'human' word. Everyone knows what 'want' means. Also, 'wanting' implies more than just motivation. 'Wanting' goes right to the heart of human urges and feelings. When there's such a powerful feeling at work helping learning to happen, little wonder that the results can be spectacular. We've all been pleasantly surprised at how well people who really want to do something usually manage to do it.

'Digesting'
This is about 'making sense' of the learning experience - and also making sense of feedback received from other people. 'Digesting' is about sorting out what is important in what's been learned. 'Digesting' is about extracting the fundamental principles from the background information. 'Digesting' is also about discarding what's not important. It's about putting things into perspective.

How real people learn

'Digesting', above all else, is about establishing a sense of *ownership* of what has been learned. It's about *far more* than the nearest word the psychologists come up with - 'reflection'.

I've now asked thousands of people the three questions we've looked at, and even got most of them to write their answers down. The people I've asked have covered all age ranges, different occupations and professions. It did not surprise me to discover that very different people still manage to learn in broadly similar ways. After all, learning is a *human* process - it matters little whether you're a human trainer, a human student or a human manager.

Wanting	motivation
Doing	Practice trial and error
Feedback	other people's reactions seeing the results
Digesting	making sense of it gaining ownership

Learning Cycles?

Probably the best known 'learning cycle' is that involving the stages 'active experimentation', 'reflective observation', 'concrete experience' and abstract conceptualisation'. One problem I have with this cycle is that it is not too clear where on the cycle one should best start - or indeed which way round to go - or even in which order the four steps should be connected - you will notice I've not included any arrows.

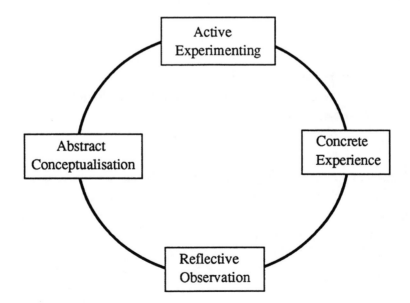

How real people learn

In fact, I think that there are times when one needs to be in two places at once in the cycle. Also, the terminology in the above cycle may mean a lot to those who think they know what it all means, but it may leave most other people quite cold. It's tempting to try drawing a cycle with 'wanting', 'doing', 'feedback' and 'digesting'. At least there seems to be an obvious logical order.

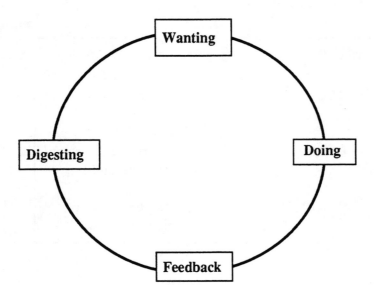

But are we really going round in circles?
Although I am keen to acknowledge the usefulness of thinking of learning as a combination of processes, I think that imposing a 'cyclic' order on learning processes is - to say the least - a gross oversimplification. In fact, the more that the four processes can be made to overlap, the better. For example:

- It's important to keep on 'wanting' while 'doing'.
- It's useful to be seeking 'feedback' while 'doing' as well as after 'doing'.
- It's useful to be continuing to seek 'feedback' while 'digesting'.
- It's useful to be continuing the 'doing' while receiving 'feedback' and while 'digesting' and progressively refining the whole process.

The 'wanting' stage needs to pervade throughout, so that 'doing' is wanted, 'feedback' is positively sought, opportunities for 'digesting' are seized, and so on. Perhaps a more sensible model would have 'wanting' at the heart, and 'feedback' coming from the outside, and 'doing' and 'digesting' occurring in an overlapping way as pictured on page 15.

How real people learn

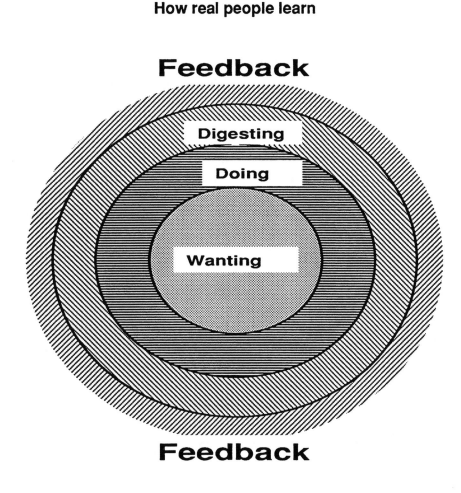

One can also imagine this as a 'spreading ripples' model, fired by the 'wanting', where the 'bounced-back' ripples from the external world constitute the 'digesting' and continue to influence the 'doing'. The main benefit of such a model is that it removes the need to think about learning as a unidirectional sequence. The model has about it both a simplicity and a complexity - in a way mirroring the simultaneous simplicity and complexity in the ways in which people actually learn.

Using the model
Probably the greatest strength of the 'wanting, doing, feedback, digesting' model of learning is that it lends itself to providing a solid foundation upon which to design educational and training programmes. If you look at any successful form of education and training, you'll find that in one way or another, all four of our ingredients of successful learning are addressed. Different situations and processes attend to each of the four in different ways.

For example, 'Wanting' is catered for by the effective face-to-face trainer or lecturer who generates enthusiasm. 'Wanting' is catered for by carefully-worded learning objectives in flexible learning materials or manuals, which capture the learners' wishes to proceed with their learning.

Learning by 'Doing' is equally at the heart of any good education or training course and in any well-designed flexible learning package.

'Feedback' is provided by tutors or trainers, or by the printed responses to exercises or self-assessment questions in flexible learning materials, or by feedback responses on-screen in computer-assisted learning programmes, or simply by fellow-learners giving feedback to each other.

The one that's all-too-easy to miss out is 'digesting'. However, all experienced tutors and trainers know how important it is to give learners the time and space to make sense of their learning and to put it into perspective. Similarly, the best learning packages cater for the fact that learners need to be given some opportunity to practise with what they've already learned, before moving on to further learning.

Conclusions

For far too long, 'learning' has been considered as a special kind of human activity, with its own jargon and vocabulary. It's not! To learn is to be human. My main point is that 'wanting', 'doing', 'feedback' and 'digesting' are so close to the essence of 'being human' that it's possible to keep these processes firmly in mind when designing educational courses, training programmes and learning resources. It's far easier to do so than to try and work out how to engender such things as 'concrete experience', 'abstract conceptualisation' or 'reflective observation', even though such terms in fact relate to no more - and no less - than 'wanting', 'doing', 'feedback' and 'digesting'.

Chapter 2

Never mind the teaching - feel the learning!

Teaching quality assessment

There's a lot of talk of this these days. Barely have the embers of the research assessment exercise died down; the discussion has switched to teaching quality. In fact, the word 'quality' has been in vogue for some time now, with 'total quality' and BS5750, and so on. What is 'quality' anyway? Everything has quality - good quality, poor quality, middling quality - you name it. We should really be using an adjective such as 'high' or 'good' in the debate about quality if it is to mean anything at all. However, in this article I want to switch the focus away from teaching quality to learning quality, and explore some adjectives and descriptors which may be more useful than simply 'good' or 'high'.

Revisiting research quality assessment

There can be few people in Higher Education who have not had a try at making sense of the research rankings and the '1s', '2s', '3s', '4s' and '5s' which emerged from the research assessment exercise. Then there are the rank orders into which departments and institutions can be placed - and the endless possibilities for re-ranking which can be engaged in by altering the formulas from which the numbers derive. Let me give a personal reflection on the meaning of 'research quality'. The first solo research paper I published bears the reference:

> Race, W P (1970) *The specific adsorption of oxalate anions at the mercury-aqueous solution interphase* Journal of Electroanalytical Chemistry, **24** 315-322

Actually, it was about my ninth paper, but the others had co-authors such as my PhD supervisor and the Professor who led the research school, so this paper counted more than my previous ones, as only my name was on it. Also, it was in a highly respectable journal of the day and in the field, with rigorous refereeing - indeed I had to adjust my grammar more than once to please the editor. It was a much better journal than 'the other one' where we published our more dubious papers. So it was a piece of 'quality research' no doubt. I still remember writing up the conclusions from my experiments - it was a neat interpretation of something that had not been observed before. The results were valid and still stand. My work was duly quoted in ensuing papers in the field till the discussion ran its course - plenty of 'citations' - but did that mean much? There was only one thing wrong (as in later life I came to realise) with that first solo paper of mine - and the rest of my papers of that time: they were not *important*. They were not going to alter the state of the art, or change people's thinking. The research may have been neat and well-written but it was of very little practical value indeed. However, in the research assessment exercise, it seems to have been exactly that kind of research which was valued. And look at how seriously the results of the research assessment exercise are being taken - used in decisions about funding, no less! It seems inescapable that the same thing will happen to 'teaching quality' rankings and ratings - but will the basic measure be just as crude once more? I fear so.

Performance indicators

This is a popular pair of words nowadays. Let's leave aside the performance indicators which may apply to research quality, or to institutional quality, or to the management of Universities and Colleges. Let's grapple with the performance indicators which may - or may not - be linked to teaching quality. Let's formulate a few for several of the aspects of the work of a teacher in higher education.

Large-Group Teaching
- Gives brilliant lectures, which change the lives of students.
- Uses professional-looking overheads, which can be clearly seen from the back.
- Prepares interesting and valuable handout materials.
- Handles questions from the class with skill and sensitivity.

Small-Group Teaching
- Provides interesting tutorials.
- Uses tutorials to deepen students' understanding of what was given in the lectures.
- Shows students how to tackle problems and how to structure their learning of the subject.
- Doesn't post a notice saying 'Tutorial cancelled today due to staff meeting'.

Assessment
- Sets coursework regularly.
- Marks coursework within a week or three.
- Sets well-worded exam questions.
- Marks exam questions and works out grades or percentages.

There are 12 to be going on with. Twelve 'performance indicators'. Will these be the sorts of things that assessors of teaching quality will be trying to measure? Actually, 'performance indicators' are apt descriptions for the things I listed above - because all of the factors above involve 'performances'. Especially when it is known that someone is sitting at the back watching my lecture, or looking over my shoulder while I set my exam questions, or examining my marked scripts for fairness and objectivity, my performance will be impeccable. Teachers are highly intelligent people and well able to put on a good performance when the occasion warrants it. But hardly anything I have said yet has any real bearing on the *quality of learning*.

Quality of learning

After all, that's what education and training are all about. The end product is people-development. This involves not only what people know, but also what they can do with it all. Moreover, let's not forget that the end product should most importantly include what people *are*. So perhaps a 'teaching quality' assessment exercise is quite futile. There can be all sorts of excellence in the ways that teachers perform (at least while being observed), without any real guarantee that there is a corresponding excellence in the quality of learning which accompanies such performances. In fact, the quality of learning is likely to depend on many things besides teaching. Here are a few things that affect quality of learning.

- quality of student accommodation;
- quality and quantity of interaction with other students;
- quality (and quantity?) of food;
- quality of the seats in lecture rooms and small-group rooms;
- quality of the stock and the service in the library;
- quality of the car-parking provision, or the public transport infrastructure.

So what is learning?

If we're going to try to define some quality criteria for learning, it will be helpful to identify some factors involved in the act of learning. How does learning happen? If you believe most of what you read about learning, you may believe that it's a combination of active experimentation, concrete experience, reflective observation and abstract conceptualisation - not necessarily in that order. In fact, it's quite hard to argue with such a model, because the terms are so vague and broad that they can mean all things to all people. My own preference, as I discussed in some detail in Chapter 1, is for a model which uses everyday words which mean more or less the same to everyone. In short, successful learning seems to require four processes to be in place. These consist of:

- *wanting* to learn (or motivation)
- *doing* - learning by practice and by trial and error
- *feedback* - finding out how it's going
- *digesting* - making sense of what's been learned.

This model of learning is in everyday language and can become a very versatile basis not only for helping learners themselves rationalise their approaches to studying, but also for helping teachers to design learning programmes and learning materials to accommodate and embrace such natural and instinctive learning processes.

Let's look at each of these in a little more detail in the context this time of quality of teaching and learning.

Wanting

Most teachers will agree that if learners really want to learn something, they will succeed. Equally, if the 'want' is missing, the probability of failure to learn is increased dramatically. Therefore, we can deduce that a 'performance indicator' for effective learning is 'the want to learn'. There are ways that this 'want' can be researched - but in the context of assessment of *teaching* quality, it's rather harder to specify a performance indicator along the lines 'enhances the *want* to learn'.

Doing

Most people agree that most learning happens in an active, 'learning by doing' mode, rather than in a passive 'being taught' mode. For example, in most traditional lectures, not much learning happens at the time. There may well be plenty of learning happening later (maybe months later, when learners get down to studying their lecture notes for an impending exam). However, perhaps the lecture should not aim at achieving 'learning by doing' to any great extent, and concentrate on amplifying the 'want' to learn.

Feedback

To feel positive about something we do, most of us depend on the reactions of other people - or feedback. This is indeed something that teachers can get involved with. They can give 'expert-witness' feedback to learners - and they often do. However, the amount of feedback that any one learner in a large class can receive is necessarily limited, so perhaps a more beneficial role of teachers can be to orchestrate feedback on a more substantial scale, for example by facilitating self-assessment and peer-assessment. The greater the amount of feedback that learners can receive *before* the end-of-course assessments, the greater their opportunity to learn from such feedback.

Digesting

I prefer this word to the 'reflection' that is often used to describe what I mean here. 'Digesting' is making sense of what has been learned, including making sense of the ways in which it was learned. But furthermore, 'digesting' is about making logical decisions about what is important enough to retain and about what is unimportant enough to be discarded. A performance indicator for successful learning could be the extent to which 'digesting' is achieved. A parallel performance indicator for related aspects of *teaching* quality is much harder to define. Teachers may well be able to help with visible cases of 'learning indigestion', but it's far less straightforward to combat the undiagnosed learning indigestion which so often finally manifests itself as a terminal condition in end-of-course examinations.

Assessment of learning quality

Although it may be difficult to translate the processes needed for successful learning into teaching quality indicators, the 'wanting, doing, feedback, digesting' model of learning is more readily translated into quality-of-learning indicators. Some of these, not surprisingly, involve teachers too. Here is a first attempt to formulate a shortlist of criteria for learning quality. I will once more restrict myself to twelve in total, to match my attempt to define some teaching quality criteria earlier in this article.

Wanting

- How well does course documentation whet the appetites of learners for what is to come in each course?
- To what extent do lectures create a desire to learn, and to what extent do tutorials and seminars reinforce the desire to learn?
- How interesting are coursework assignments and laboratory experiments as ways of helping learners to maintain their desire to continue to learn?

Doing

- How well is it explained to learners that their task is not just to memorise the knowledge base of each subject, but to gain the ability to apply it?
- How well does coursework help learners to realise the benefits of learning-by-doing?
- How well is 'trial and error' used deliberately as a productive way of learning suitable things in an atmosphere where error is seen by learners as constructive rather than demoralising?

Feedback

- Apart from grades and scores (which are feedback in their own right), how well is feedback *discussion* given to learners, for example by written comments on their assessed work, or face-to-face discussions about their work?
- How fully are the benefits of learners giving feedback to each other (for example in informal peer-assessment) exploited?
- How well are learners guided in the benefits to them of seeking feedback proactively and of using critical feedback constructively?

Digesting

- Are learners alerted to the need to pause every so often and make sense of what they have learned, rather than to rush ahead trying to learn yet more?
- Are coursework assignments and experimental work structured to help learners to make sense of the theories and concepts to which they have been introduced?
- Are learners helped to see the benefits they can derive from each other, for example by explaining things to each other, as a way of helping them make sense of what they have learned?

Conclusions

If the learning is alright, the teaching will look after itself. I believe that the criteria I have presented for successful learning are far more worthy of application than those I suggested for successful teaching. In short, it will be much more productive to investigate the quality of learning than to probe the quality of teaching as such. Indeed, when teaching is designed in such a way as to maximise the quality of learning, then we are talking about teaching of 'high quality'. Such teaching goes a long way beyond the 'polished performances' which we can all deliver on demand - and which may only marginally affect the quality of learning.

Chapter 3

Developing competence

Abstract

In the late 1980s and early 1990s, education and training have become increasingly preoccupied with 'competence'. A bewildering amount of paperwork has been built round competence statements, performance criteria, elements of competence, range statements, and other descriptors of intended learning outcomes. This chapter is an attempt to bring the discussion back to **people.** In this chapter, I propose simple 'definitions' for competence (and the lack of competence), and I provide some suggestions about how learners - and teachers - may be helped to acquire a positive feeling of **ownership** of the competences they develop.

What is 'competence'?

'Competence' has become the buzz-word of the early 90s in training and education (in the same way that 'open learning' was the buzz-phrase of the 80s). What does 'competence' mean? Attempts to define competence abound - but in general seem to cause confusion by their diversity. Perhaps sometimes competence means something similar to 'capability'. Perhaps sometimes competence means something more specific - ability to do, ability to perform, ability to make judgments, ability to decide, ability to take responsibility, and on and on! Or maybe competence means a whole range of such abilities?

There is a simple solution: **competence = can do.**

This allows **any** kind of competence - from the simplest to the most complex - to be expressed in suitable terms. A competence statement becomes a **'can do'** statement. This is better than a 'will do' statement in that it retains the choice of the individual. It is important that people feel **ownership** of the competences they develop - describing competence in terms of 'can do' statements adds to such a feeling.

Measuring competence

When competence is inadequately described, (for example, by vagueness in the wording of competence statements), it becomes in danger of being one of those things where 'you know it if you see it'. If competence statements are vague, it becomes hard to see how we may measure competence. There is then a tendency to think 'if we can't measure it, it doesn't exist'. But at the same time, if competence is not properly described, when trying to measure it the wrong things may be measured - leading to the feeling 'if you **can** measure it, it isn't **IT'**.

How can competence be measured? It needs to be measured in some way if credit is to be awarded for having it. It may be difficult to measure particular competences directly - we can measure what people **do** - we can measure what people **have done** - but that does not necessarily mean we've measured what they **can do.** Nor does it necessarily refer to what they **will** do. However, the **result** of competence being exercised is often measurable. Such results can take many forms - actions, products, judgments, ideas, decisions, and so on. Since **results** are needed to measure competence, let's call them **evidence.** Evidence can of course take a multitude of forms - one piece of evidence may reflect several competences - or it may take several pieces of evidence to reflect a single competence.

The reverse of competence?

The word **incompetence** comes to mind. Unfortunately, this word carries overtones - it is usually taken to mean something more sinister than 'can't yet do'. What would be your reaction if someone referred to you as 'incompetent'?

Perhaps we can look at it like this: **incompetence = can't** *ever* **do.**

Uncompetence!

Let's adopt this word to get over the problems with the word 'incompetence'. **Uncompetence** can have a number of meanings without the degrading overtones of incompetence. Uncompetence can incorporate choices, making it easier to feel ownership. (No-one would want to own incompetence!)

> uncompetence = **can't** *yet* **do**
> uncompetence = **don't** *need* **to do**
> uncompetence = **don't** *want* **to do**
> uncompetence = *won't* **do**

The word 'uncompetence', when explained as above, is not threatening or insulting to people. Most people willingly accept that they have 'uncompetences' of various sorts, in each of the categories above.

Levels of competence

It's easy enough to express competences in terms of **'can do'** statements. It is more difficult to describe **how competent.** The level of competence may depend on several things, eg.

- the requirements of the job
- other people's assessments of competence
- the particular dimensions chosen for its measurement.

It would be useful if we could define some sort of **'absolute'** competence which was completely independent of assessment - formative or summative. After all, people can so often be highly competent at something - but not prove so in assessment. This is - of course - the fault of the process of assessment or of the content being assessed. If someone were to have 'absolute' competence, this should be reflected by any valid kind of assessment.

However, we can think of some sort of scale of competence, spanning several levels.

highly competent	(can do very well)
quite competent	(can do quite well)
neither competent nor uncompetent	(can just about do)
rather uncompetent	(can't really yet do - but nearly)
highly uncompetent	(e.g. can't yet do at all)

For the purposes of argument, we could imagine an arbitrary borderline between states of competence and uncompetence. The borderline has to be an arbitrary one however - if the requirement is to be **highly** competent at something, the borderline would sensibly lie between 'quite' and 'highly'.

Conscious or unconscious?

Let's think of any manifestation of competence - from a simple specific one (for example solving a mathematical equation) to a broad complex one (for example delivering a training programme). Does the owner of the competence **know about it?** Or is it unconscious?

By 'conscious' I mean 'knowing', and by 'unconscious' I mean 'unknowing' or 'subconscious' or 'unrealised'. I chose to use a scale of unconscious/conscious in the discussion which follows (rather than a knowing/unknowing scale) as I wanted to avoid the danger of getting into cognitive-psychomotor-affective discussions! Competences can be conscious or unconscious in any such domain - and (as in real life!) in complex overlaps of all three. The range from unconscious to conscious can be regarded as another scale perhaps extending as follows:

deeply unconscious	quite unconscious	on the brink of being conscious	quite conscious	acutely conscious

As before, any borderline should be regarded as arbitrary - depending on all sorts of things:

- personal perceptions, self awareness
- help from other people
- evidence - for example, assessment data.

Conscious and unconscious competence and uncompetence

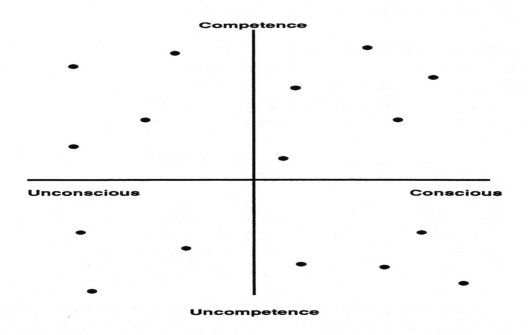

This gives us a way of mapping competence - conscious and unconscious. I should emphasise that I don't see people 'inhabiting' particular boxes, rather owning an array of different competences which at any moment in time are scattered through ALL the boxes. Most points on the diagram are perfectly alright wherever they are - no need or reason to move them. **Purposeful learning** may be regarded as moving and developing particular competences in a planned way - or acquiring such competences as may be needed for particular purposes.

Conscious competence

This is the box in which we may want to have particular competences - those to do with our jobs, our interests - and our lives in general. All good teachers wish their learners to develop particular competences in this box. Whatever the description of the competence - whatever the form of the evidence - we want it to be 'good' and we want it to be **known** that it's good.

In the context of learning or self-development, conscious competence is the **target** box. I hesitate to call it the 'objective' box or the 'aim' box - aims and objectives may only describe **part** of the competence being sought.

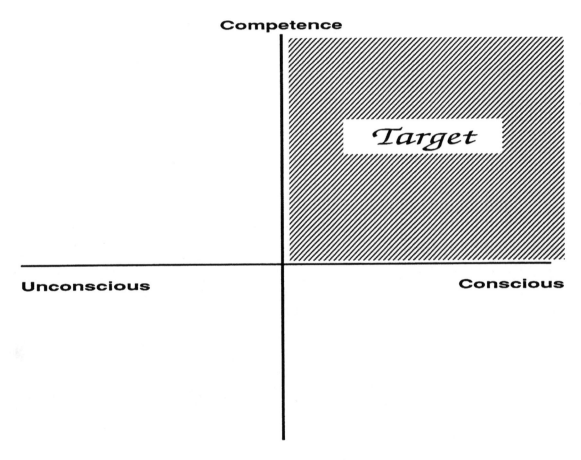

Owners of competences already in the **target** box can say or feel:
- I can do it and I **know** I can do it.
- This is one of my strengths.

People who have developed an array of conscious competences are likely to be in a position where it should not be hard to put together a collection of **evidence** on the basis of which credit may be awarded.

Conscious uncompetence

Let's call this the **transit** box. This is because if we have things in this box we're normally either on our way to getting them to the **target** box or we're quite happy to leave them where they are - for example competences we don't want - or don't need to develop. Only those uncompetences which are to be the basis for learning are the ones 'in transit'. All the rest - along with being unable to build a pyramid single-handed - may safely remain in this box.

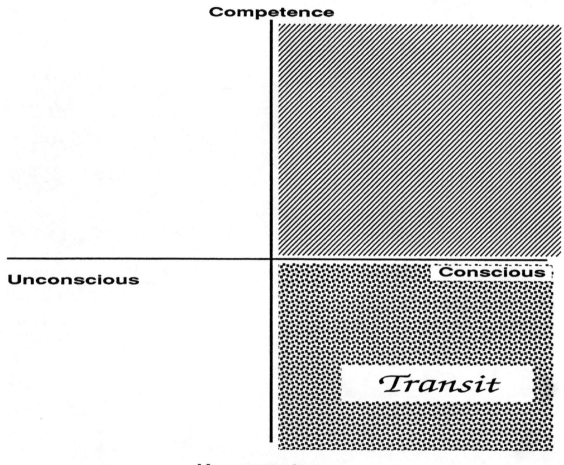

Having explained that 'it's OK to be consciously uncompetent' ask a group of learners (for example) 'how many of you are consciously uncompetent at preparing a report?' - many will identify themselves. As far as learning is concerned, conscious uncompetence is a healthy position to be in. People who know exactly what they can't yet do are usually well on the way to becoming able to do it - or at least are receptive to help in learning about it.

It's often a sensible learning strategy to deliberately address conscious uncompetence areas - that's what goes under the name of **revision** before exams - little point learning what's already been mastered!

Unconscious uncompetence

On the whole, people with things in the **transit** position can move them towards the **target** state - with or without a little help. It's worth planning the journey with some care, so that suitable **evidence** may be accumulated on the way and in due course the competences can be accredited. But **Unconscious** uncompetence is not so simple! 'Hands up those of you who are unconsciously uncompetent?' - this is a question which should get no replies! 'How many of you **know someone** who is unconsciously uncompetent?' gets a vigorous response and some mirth usually. Unconscious uncompetence is the **danger** box.

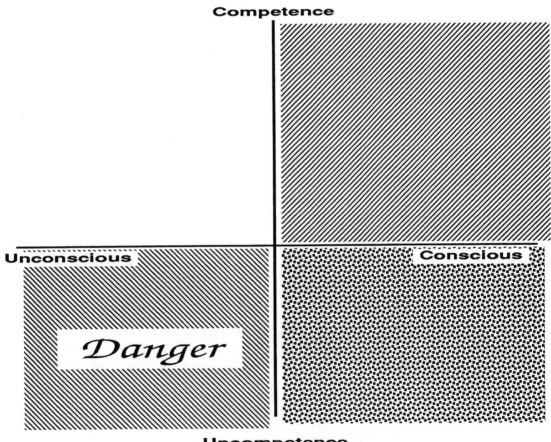

This, however, is the **danger** box only if **relevant** and **necessary** competences lie there. It then represents the problem of 'not knowing what you don't know'. If this is not sorted out, the unconscious uncompetence may continue till it is **found out** one way or another - in an exam, in poor job performance, and so on. We need to do everything we can to help people move important uncompetences from the **danger** box to the **transit** box. On entry to a programme of study, a friendly 'assessment' can help to do this - though care needs to be taken to ensure that this is not seen as a 'punitive' or 'threatening' exercise. 'Assessment' is not the friendliest of words - nor are 'diagnostic test' or 'pretest'. The benefits to learners of identifying their elements of unconscious uncompetence need to be spelled out very convincingly to get their wholehearted cooperation in seeking them out.

Self-assessment is particularly good at allowing people the comfort of privacy while they seek out their unconscious uncompetences. Thereafter, **peer-assessment** practised regularly can feel less threatening than formal assessment - and can add a feeling of companionship in some of the unconscious uncompetences discovered. In both self- and peer-assessment, learners usually benefit if provided with a suitable level of ongoing support - for example help in defining the criteria **they** can then apply to their own work. Learners who have benefited from self-assessment and/or peer-assessment will be able to see how **past** unconscious uncompetence was discovered - and, when relevant, rectified. They then become more willing to use such processes to identify **present** dangers.

Unconscious competence

This is the **magic** box. Mature learners in particular have an array of competences they don't know about. Their life experience can often be very valuable for their task of future learning. The more we can help learners **find out** about the competences they have already accrued - the more confident they feel about their ability to succeed. It has been said that the single most important factor which predetermines success is **confidence.** A quick way to develop confidence is to identify some of the relevant unconscious competences that learners have and place them firmly in the **target** box.

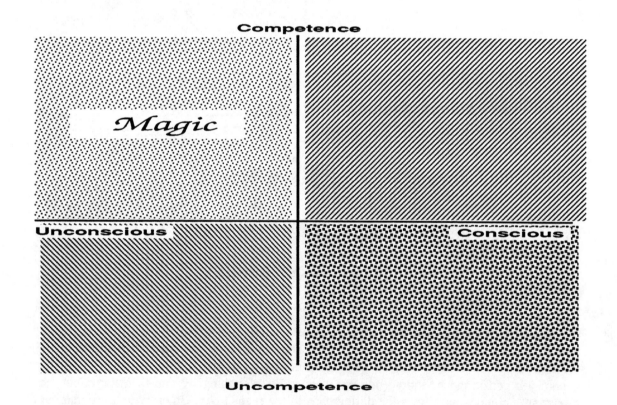

Evidence for unconscious competences may already exist - for example a learner who has already produced excellent reports may not have realised how many competences were involved in the process. Even in the absence of ready evidence, it may be quite straightforward to collect some - allowing what were unconscious competences to be accredited.

Losing competence

We've been thinking about routes leading to **gain** in competence - but it can be lost too. Take for example the ability to drive (or to teach?). After passing the driving test - and after a bit more practice - the skills involved are probably well into the **target** box. After a few years perhaps, the competence may still be there - possibly at an even higher level - but less conscious (the **magic** box). Or perhaps the skills deteriorate - albeit subconsciously - and fall into the **danger** box. (I see a lot of **evidence** of this!).

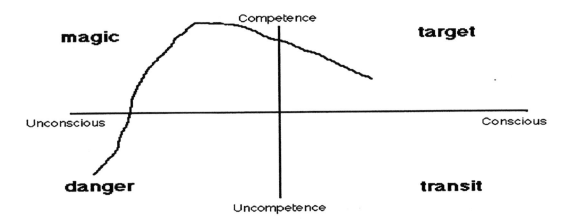

Perhaps with driving - and many other skills and competences, **regular testing** is needed to restore (or maintain) not just competence, but awareness. This analogy can be extended into many aspects of education and training. Regular updating, in-service training, professional development, appraisal - all can help clarify which competences are in which box.

Time - a third dimension?

So far, we've been looking at our model without considering the dimension of time. A map of competences and uncompetences is in a way only a snapshot - the picture is always changing. Some points will stay fixed (the 'don't need to do' and 'don't want to do' uncompetences for example). Learning, however, will involved planned **trajectories** on a three-dimensional model. Naturally, there will be many possible trajectories between a starting position (for example at a point in the **transit** box - or even more remote: the **danger** box) and a desired end-position in the **target** box. Developing effective **learning skills** will be an important aid to being able to choose and use direct trajectories.

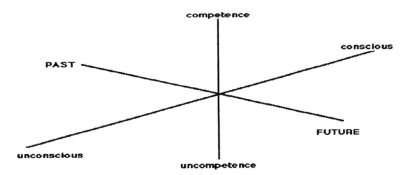

Processes leading towards competence

Not all competences can be expressed in a straightforward way. 'Can teach effectively' or 'Can learn efficiently' are far too vague to be useful competence statements as they stand. To make competences clear, they need to be linked to a range of other parameters - such as:

- performance descriptions
- performance criteria
- indicators relating to different levels of performance

The danger is, however, that the clarifications become self-defeating, by becoming so rigid or expansive that they end up in trivialising the competences they were intended to promote. In examples which I quote later in this chapter, you may decide for yourself whether or not the clarification has gone too far.

Helping learners make sense of competence
- *What exactly am I expected to become able to do?*
- *How best can I get to a suitable 'can do' state?*

The list which follows shows several key questions that learners need to address.

What do learners need to know?

- how does this particular competence fit into the context of my studies? Why is it important?

- how much does it 'count for'?

- what exactly is it that I need to become able to do? Give me an example of what it's like to have developed the competence. Can I already do it?

- how will I be expected to demonstrate the competence?

- what will constitute evidence that I have developed the competence?

- how can I tell whether I have reached the state of being able to demonstrate the competence?

- what criteria will be used to measure my competence?

Developing competence

- Syllabus objectives often give an idea of the sort of standards to be aimed towards - but often in language that is more appropriate to teachers than learners - and some times in language which would frighten off all but the most confident of learners.

- Past exam papers can provide an example of some of the things learners should become able to do. However, these too can be frightening if seen too early.

- Competence statements are in similar danger at times. It's all very well to describe successful performance in terms of the competence that it demonstrates, but it is the PERFORMANCE that is easier for the learner to anticipate - not necessarily the competence. The following example shows how competence statements can be translated into performance terms.

Standard of competence =

- **an element of competence**
- **a range statement**
- **performance criteria**

Element: promote the sale of products and services to potential customers

Performance Criteria:

- **appropriate and accurate information about the company is offered**

- **potential customer needs and status are identified accurately and politely.**

- **advantages and benefits of becoming a customer are described clearly and accurately**

- Another alternative is exposure to learners who have already gained competence. 'Proctoring' is a term used to describe (for example) final-year learners working with first-year learners on particular parts of a learning programme. The 'proctors' probably gain a lot of competence by helping their less-competent colleagues! The proctors provide evidence of how it is to have gained competence.

Spelling out the evidence

As far as printed words are concerned, I suggest that the best way of alerting learners to what's expected of them is to accompany each competence statement by one or more examples of evidence.

These examples need to avoid prescribing too much the way in which the competence can be demonstrated. Learners need freedom so that the ways in which they develop and demonstrate each competence can be as relevant as possible to their job, profession or career.

Both evidence and competence statements may need extra detail - description and specification. **Description** - especially of the sort of evidence which may be gathered - should be understandable to learners who have not yet gained a given competence. Though **Specification** may or may not be understandable to learners at this stage, it should be available to them as a means in due course of seeing exactly what sort of criteria may be applied to the evidence they produce.

Both descriptions and specifications can therefore be regarded as bridges between competence and evidence.

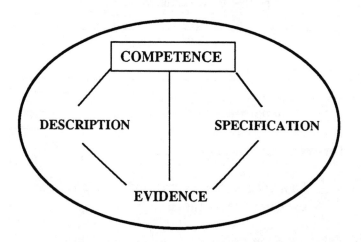

The examples which follow show how particular levels of performance can be identified, so that learners can work out for themselves how their competence is developing with reference to the standards against which it will be assessed.

Example 1: problem-solving competences

Appreciation

> **Problem-Solving: Establishing aims, recognising and evaluating relevant and essential factors**

5	**Apprecition of tasks is rapid and almost faultless. Consistently identifies the best solution.**
4	**Establishes aims promptly and recognises most of the relevant factors and all of the essential factors. Evaluation produces efficient and practical solutions.**
3	**Establishes aims corrently, and with minor prompting identifies some of the relevant factors and all of the essential factors. Evaluation is somewhat hesitant, but usually achieves an acceptable solution.**
2	**Is slow to establish aims. Usually requires assistance to identify some of the relevant and essential factors. Has difficulty in evaluating problems and solutions and solutions are often unsound.**
1	**Has only a vague idea of the aims and is totally unable to evaluate relevant factors or to produce any reasonable solutions.**

The marks '1' to '5' can be awarded according to the level to which the relevant skills are demonstrated. If competence statements are to be successful as a way of describing standards, learners need these extra degrees of information - examples of the factors by which the standards may be recognised and measured once they have been achieved. This points to increased dialogue between learners (individually and in groups) and their teachers or trainers - which can profitably replace some (perhaps all?) of the time normally used in trainers 'transmitting' and learners 'receiving'. The example below gives a further view of how a 'can do' competence (in this case oral communication in the context of telephone skills and interview technique) can be illustrated using performance measures.

Example 2: Telephone and interview competences

Oral communication

> **Power of spoken expression: effectiveness
> of interviews and telephone technique**

---

5   Has a gift of lucid and fluid expression. Invariably adopts the most appropriate tone and manner. Interviews are well structured, with a very good question technique.

4   Is able to be understood without difficulty. Adopts an appropriate tone and manner. Interview structure and question techniques are sound.

3   Some difficulty in expressing ideas, occasionally adopts an inappropriate tone or manner. Interviews are effective despite some weakness in structure or question technique.

2   Considerable difficulty in expressing ideas. Often adopts an inappropriate tone or manner. Interviews are inadequately structured with poor question technique.

1   Lacks any ability to express ideas clearly. Tone and manner are mostly inappropriate. Interviews have no recognisable structure and question technique is inappropriate.

To reach a stable 'can do' position, it is usual to have gone through *'have done often'* states. For a competence to be fully developed, however, it needs to be demonstrable that it is 'done often' - for learners and teachers this means performance-assessment and appraisal, respectively. If the people whose competence is being measured are aware of the criteria *before* they are assessed, they can consciously develop their skills to meet each of the criteria.

Competence and strengths, weaknesses, opportunities, threats

Another set of variables - or a means of assisting the *processes* of competence development? 'SWOT' analysis has long been used as an aid to helping people find out where they are, and how best to go on from there. Having addressed the question 'what exactly am I expected to become able to do' by identifying the sort of evidence which may be required for assessment, it can be productive to lead learners (particularly in groups) through SWOT analysis. One way of applying SWOT analysis is to use sheets with four boxes into which learners write their own feelings about each of the aspects involved in the context (for example) of their planned learning programmes.

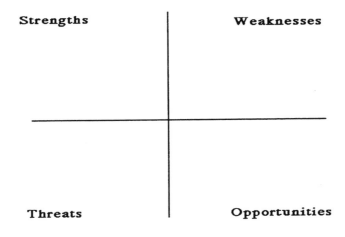

Strengths	**Weaknesses**
Threats	**Opportunities**

- **Strengths** - 'things you know you're good at already' - are a start for things belonging to the **target** box - they're conscious competences. Evidence may already be available, or may be collected relatively easily.

- **Weaknesses** - 'things you know you're not yet good at' - can be regarded as conscious uncompetences - things presently in the **transit** box. Some will matter - and need to move towards the **target** box. Others won't matter at all and can remain where they are. The kinds of evidence that will demonstrate that chosen weaknesses have been overcome can be planned, so that (where needed or wanted) progression to demonstrable competence can be achieved as efficiently as possible.

- **Opportunities** - (for example) 'your answers to the question 'what's in it for me?'' - are more complex. They could be the chance to move things into the **target** box - both from the unconscious competences (**magic**) box and from the unconscious uncompetence (**danger**) box (i.e. to overcome the danger by first finding out about it, then rectifying it).

- **Threats** - (for example) 'things that could stop you getting there' - also are more complex. One of the threats could be the shock of discovering things in the **danger** box. Another threat could be not knowing things in the **magic** box - things which could be employed to lead to successful learning. Perhaps the most significant threat could be 'lost competence' - far better to anticipate such a threat and plan accordingly, than to find out too late that a particular previous competence is now absent.

Competent teaching

In the case of professional skills such as 'teaching', 'managing' and 'leading', it can be even more difficult to express competences in a simple format. For example, suppose the following competences were to be sought in teachers:

- can use self- and peer- assessment to promote students' learning
- can design flexible or open learning resources
- can work effectively with both large groups and small groups of students

A considerable amount of additional detail is needed before the real meaning of such statements is clarified. For example, the *processes* involved in designing flexible or open learning resources could be spelled out as follows:

- identifying part of a syllabus which lends itself to open or flexible learning
- researching the quality and availability of any existing open or flexible learning packages in the subject area
- expressing part of the syllabus in terms of learning objectives and performance outcomes
- devising self-assessment questions and responses
- producing an open or flexible learning package, or adapting and improving an existing one
- piloting the open learning package and gathering feedback from students
- measuring students' achievement of the objectives and their demonstration of the performance outcomes
- editing and adjusting the package in the light of feedback from students

The broader area of *'teaching competences'* could be elaborated as follows:

- identifying which topics lend themselves to:
  - large-group presentations or lectures
  - student-led seminars or discussions
  - tutorials
  - practical or field work
  - student project work
  - student team work

from a breakdown of part of a syllabus into learning objectives, performance outcomes and assessment criteria
- identifying criteria for the successful use of each of the teaching-learning methods selected
- conducting or facilitating a range of teaching-learning methods, collecting evidence of each in an appropriate manner
- collecting and analysing student feedback about each of the teaching-learning methods employed

From 'can do' towards 'does do'

The illustration below shows some elements of 'competence' relating to dealing with large groups of students. These elements were devised by a small group of lecturers, who then 'weighted' each of the elements. This provided them with a way of addressing the relative importance of the different competences. The list was turned into a self-appraisal device by adding the various columns on the right hand side of the figure.

Some Competences for large-group sessions which foster effective learning	do often	do some-times	can do	don't yet do	can't yet do	don't need to do	don't wish to do
• gives students the chance to learn from each other 6,2,0,2,4,1 **15**							
• avoids irritating repetitions, e.g. 'um' 0,1,0,1,0,2 **4**							
• 'sets up stall' at beginning (markets, creates expectations) 6,2,2,0,0,3 **13**							
• doesn't read (i.e. read out aloud from books, notes, etc) 0,3,0,2,0,2 **7**							
• identifies purposes and expected outcomes 6,1,2,2,3,1 **15**							
• encourages useful contributions 6,2,1,1,4,3 **17**							
• listens to students' contributions 0,2,1,2,1,1 **7**							
• uses student expertise 0,3,0,1,2,2 **8**							
(numbers are individuals' weightings out of 30 points, followed by 'group weighting' (bold) out of 180 points)							

Beyond competence - towards excellence?

The most serious flaw in the competence debate is that it is not easy to see where there is room in the model to excel. It is all very well to aim to make people competent - but civilisation has advanced through the work of people who were more than competent. Such people did more than reach a 'can do' state regarding things that were already known - they achieved a 'did first' state in things which were previously unknown.

This will be the downfall of the competence era. While the competence model will work as long as we wish to ensure that people reach a *minimum* level of ability, we need room in our education and training provision for fostering the attainment of new levels of competence - and unthought-of competence indicators and forms of evidence.

Conclusions

Much of this section has been about helping people 'find out where they're at', as a basis for moving on to developing those competences that **they** need, and producing the evidence **we** need to accredit their performance. It has also been about giving learners a feeling of ownership for the competences they develop and the processes they employ to do so. In a similar way, competences involved in teaching can be identified and clarified, and the same sort of ownership can be built in to self-appraisal tools. My suggestion is that we help our learners to gain a day-to-day perspective of the development of their competences, rather than waiting for some day of judgment on which they will find out - maybe too late. Similarly, competences connected with our teaching should be addressed and developed systematically - rather than letting things ride until some external agent finds them lacking.

Chapter 4

Quality of assessment

Abstract

What our learners *really* pay for (or what society pays us for) are their Degrees or their Diplomas or their Certificates. Yet we put much more emphasis on trying to teach our students than we normally put into designing assessment - particularly the 'formal assessment' that counts towards final qualifications. Assessment is where learners often get a raw deal. In this chapter, I will propose the following ten 'worries' about assessment, and explore ways of leading to a better quality of assessment.

Ten worries about assessment

1   Assessment is often done in a rush, to meet exam board deadlines. It's rarely done under the best of conditions!

2   Assessment is often done by bored people, tired of reading the same answers to the same questions (and seeing the same mistakes).

3   Assessment tends to be governed by 'what is easy to assess'. Therefore, traditional written exams (relatively straightforward to assess) are used. These measure students' skills at tackling traditional written exams.

4   Students rarely know the intimate details of the assessment criteria, and how we interpret them.

5   How should we develop students' *unassessable* qualities? Should we refrain from developing them because we can't measure them?

6   Almost all assessment processes in common use foster student competition rather than collaboration. No wonder our educated people are so bad at working in teams.

7   What competences are measured by assessment anyway? Are they 'can do' competences? Or are they simply 'did do, once' ghosts?

8   If we were to introduce 'Quality in Assessment BS5750A what should the criteria look like? What evidence of competence should *assessors* demonstrate?

9   'If you can't measure it, it doesn't exist. If you can measure it, it isn't *it*'. What should we be trying to measure?

10 Where stops the buck? Whose fault is it that assessment is so artificial? HoDs? Employers? Assessors? Validators? The Government? Yours? Mine?

Is Competence enough?

In 1991, the Association of Educational and Training Technology (AETT) International Conference had the theme 'Developing and Measuring Competence'. As one of the editors of the proceedings of that conference (Saunders and Race, 1992), I became well acquainted with the many views on competence which were aired by the various contributors. It was heartening to see that many of the approaches to the development of competence focused on defining the *evidence* which would be sufficient to demonstrate competence.

However, I was left with some concerns about whether competence would often end up as *minimum* competence rather than *high* competence. Also, I already hinted at some of my concerns towards the close of the previous chapter. The following two figures pose some questions about 'shades' of competence, and about a range of descriptors which may be needed to provide more information than simply 'can do'.

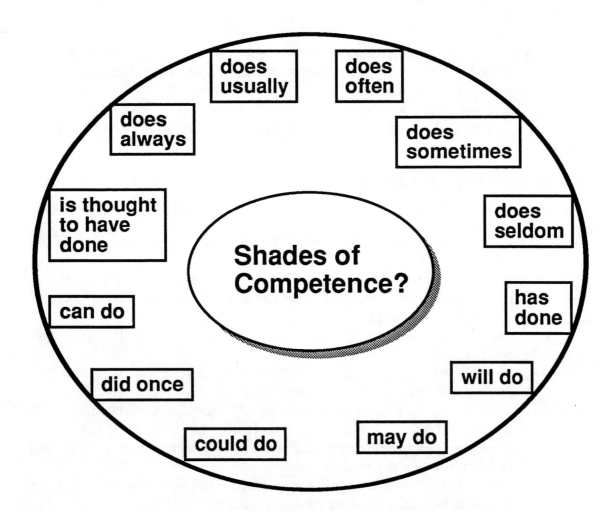

Figure 1. *Shades of Competence*

Quality of assessment

Figure 2. *Some competence descriptors*

Towards mass higher education

Higher education in the United Kingdom is being moved 'in fits and starts' towards greater participation rates, despite apparent U-turns in Government fiscal policies on expansion. In the long term, for all sorts of reasons - and at whatever cost - the pressures for higher participation rates in higher and further education will be irresistible. This means not only rapidly increasing numbers of school leavers, but also many more non-traditional entrants. Already, many lecturers and tutors are seeking help in handling large classes. It is clear that the workload of staff in higher education is increasing, as they become responsible for more and more learners.

In some ways, teaching can be 'done to' large numbers almost as easily as to small numbers - it's almost as easy to lecture to 300 as to lecture to 100. However, teaching greater numbers may have little connection with learning by greater numbers. And when it comes to assessment, there are no short cuts. It usually takes three times the amount of time to assess 300 learners as it would to assess 100 learners. The main challenge we face as we move towards a mass higher education system is merely maintaining the quality of assessment we presently have - not to mention improving it.

Assessment and learning: how do they mix?

In Chapter 1 I introduced the simple model of learning summarised again below:

- *wanting* to learn (motivation)
- learning by *doing* (practice, learning from mistakes, and so on)
- learning through *feedback* (to develop positive *feelings* about the learning)
- *digesting* (taking stock, making sense of the experience, and of the feedback).

How does assessment usually relate to these steps in the learning process? Let's take the most common form of assessment - the written examination.

- **wanting to learn (motivation):** Not many people like exams! The fact that there is an exam coming along at the end of the road is not the strongest motivator for most people. The inevitability of traditional forms of assessment is a key factor in preventing many people from participating in learning. Assessment processes are at cross purposes with learning processes.

- **learning by *doing* (practice, learning from mistakes, and so on):** Learning by doing can indeed happen during assessments, including written exams. Mistakes are indeed made during assessment - plenty of them! But learning by doing *while being assessed* is hardly the best way of using experiential learning. Besides, it is usually presumed that the learning should have taken place *before* the assessment event. Again, assessment processes are at cross purposes with learning processes.

- **learning through *feedback* (to develop positive *feelings* about the learning):** All assessment results in some sort of feedback. However, it's often the absolute minimum of feedback - for example a mere score - and that weeks or months after the event! There is little or no real feedback, and chances to learn from the feedback are minimal. Once more, assessment processes are at cross purposes with learning processes.

- **digesting (taking stock, making sense of the experience, and of the feedback):** Exams are better known for producing *indigestion* than for allowing people the chance to consolidate their learning. As I've said, the feedback is usually very limited in scope (and often delayed in time) and is not a useful means towards 'digesting'. Such feedback as there is, tends to be one-way feedback. There's little or no chance to discuss the details or negotiate what best to do next. Yet again, assessment processes are at cross purposes with learning processes.

Perhaps traditional forms of assessment have only one real contribution towards learning - people are frightened (shamed) into doing some learning so that they may minimise their chances of being shown to be 'lacking'. Much intensive learning is done just before exams - but most of it is of a superficial nature and soon forgotten again.

Ten worries - and some suggestions

In my Abstract at the start of this Chapter, I listed ten worries I have about assessment. I would like now to repeat them, giving a little more detail about my concerns, and offering some suggestions about how the problems may be minimised. Many of my suggestions point towards involving learners in their own assessment. This can be achieved by letting learners get their hands on the assessment criteria. It can be achieved even better by letting learners *apply* the assessment criteria, in self-assessment and peer-assessment. It is achieved *best* by helping learners to *formulate* the criteria, then apply them. An illustrated discussion of uses of self- and peer-assessment is given later in this chapter.

1   *Assessment is often done in a rush, to meet exam board deadlines. It's rarely done under the best of conditions!*

This is because assessment tends to be done to learners - not by them. Assessment tends to be done at the end of learning something, rather than as a means to help the learning processes. In public exams, examiners often face piles of some hundreds of scripts, which all need to be finished within only a week or two.

Suggestions:

- allow much more time for assessment, so that it can be done well.
- allow learners to use self- and peer-assessment, so they can learn by assessing.
- set questions or tasks where there will not be too many ways for learners to interpret them, making it easier to assess their work, and giving you more time to assess it objectively.

2   *Assessment is often done by bored people, tired of reading the same answers to the same questions (and seeing the same mistakes).*

Examiners get thoroughly fed-up as they wade through hundreds of scripts. They get discouraged when they see things they hoped their learners would have mastered, only to find that messages have not got across. Any tedious or repetitive task causes people to change their mood. If assessors' moods plunge, the objectivity of assessment is likely to be affected accordingly.

Suggestions:

- decrease the emphasis on traditional written exams altogether.
- allow *learners* to learn by reading their own mistakes, and those of their peers.
- 'double-blind' marking is expensive, but will make assessment more objective, not just because of the second-opinion, but also because of the effect of being a little more careful to mark objectively because of the likelihood of subjectivity being detected!

Quality of assessment

3   *Assessment tends to be governed by 'what is easy to assess'. Therefore, traditional written exams (relatively straightforward to assess) are used. These measure learners' skills at tackling traditional written exams.*

There is still not enough attention being paid to what should constitute the *evidence* upon which to base awards. Many important competences are simply not assessable by traditional methods. While it is perfectly possible to use traditional methods to measure recall of facts and information, it is not-at-all easy to use such methods to measure innovation, judgment, or personality. Fig.3 shows an overhead transparency I use to alert students to the various agendas that may be served by traditional exams.

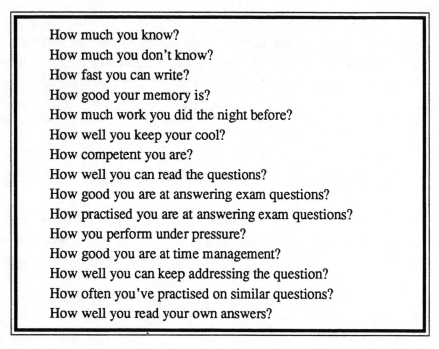

How much you know?
How much you don't know?
How fast you can write?
How good your memory is?
How much work you did the night before?
How well you keep your cool?
How competent you are?
How well you can read the questions?
How good you are at answering exam questions?
How practised you are at answering exam questions?
How you perform under pressure?
How good you are at time management?
How well you can keep addressing the question?
How often you've practised on similar questions?
How well you read your own answers?

Figure 3. *What exams measure?*

Suggestions:

- look carefully at exactly what is being measured by each form of assessment.
- refrain from measuring the same things all the time - especially recall. People who can *find* and *apply* information are usually more valuable than people who simply happen to remember a lot of it.
- discuss with your learners exactly what you are going to try and measure, so they can prepare in a well-focused way for assessment.

Quality of assessment

4   *Learners rarely know the intimate details of the assessment criteria, and how we interpret them.*

There really is no excuse for this. The *reason* may be sinister - that those who design the assessment criteria are not sufficiently confident about them to show them to the learners! Assessors often fear that learners may demand to know 'why did I get 65% for this, when my friend got 75%?' Surely, they have every right to ask this sort of question - and to learn from the feedback they should be given by way of a response to the question.

Suggestions:

- give learners the opportunity not only to see the intimate details of assessment criteria, but also to *use* the criteria.
- as a class exercise, get learners to apply a past assessment framework to specimen past answers, then to compare scores or grades, and discuss the reasons for differences.
- get learners to design an assessment framework for a given task and give them feedback about the objectivity and practicality of the assessment criteria they devise.

5   *How should we develop learners' unassessable qualities? Should we refrain from developing them because we can't measure them?*

'Don't bother to learn anything, when you can't see how they can ask you about it at the end of the day': this is a perfectly rational view taken by learners, deciding what to learn and what not to learn.

Suggestions:

- bring the unassessable qualities firmly onto the agenda. Explain to learners why they're important and work out with learners what kinds of *evidence* can be linked to these qualities, and how the demonstration of that evidence can be built in to assessment procedures.
- devise assessed tasks of the sort where learners *necessarily* develop desirable qualities *en route* to an assessed piece of work. For example, assess a 'learning log' of reflections on participation in a team project, as a means to cause learners to develop their collaborative skills and to reflect on them.

6   *Almost all assessment processes in common use foster learner competition rather than collaboration. No wonder our educated people are so bad at working in teams.*

Learners preparing for exams are often quite secretive about the work they do. No-one likes to be thought of as 'a swot'! However, it's more sinister than this: we actually *compound* the competition by using norm-referenced assessment far too much. In other words, only a certain proportion of learners are allowed to receive 'A' grades, or 1st-class Honours degree classifications. Therefore, learners *are* in competition.

Quality of assessment

Suggestions:

- use criterion-referenced assessment only - abolish the use of norm-referencing.
- help learners to feel that they can help each other prepare to demonstrate their competence, without disadvantaging one another.
- build-in *group* tasks to the overall assessment plan. For example, allow members of a group to agree on how to split up the tutor-assessed overall mark for the product of the work of the group.

7   *What competences are measured by assessment anyway? Are they 'can do' competences? Or are they simply 'did do, once' ghosts?*

Exams tend to measure 'did once' competences. At their worst, they still measure 'knew once' competences rather than 'did once'!

Suggestions:

- increase the proportion of assessment schedules allocated to continuous assessment - which measure 'is doing' competences rather than 'did once' ones.
- involve learners in self-assessment and peer-assessment of traditional-type exams (with due moderation where necessary). This at least allows learners to benefit from the learning payoff associated with reflecting on their own (and each other's) triumphs and disasters - better than just receiving a good or bad grade.

8   *If we were to introduce 'Quality in Assessment BS5750A what should the criteria look like? What evidence of competence should assessors demonstrate?*

At present, it is automatically assumed that anyone appointed to a post involving teaching or lecturing is blessed with all the skills needed to design assessment schemes and implement fair assessment. People are appointed to teaching (and assessing) posts not on the basis of how well they can do either task, but often on the record of their own academic performance.

Suggestions:

- assess the assessors. Have a system of 'licences' to assess, and police the system thoroughly. Moves in this direction are already underway in the world of training.
- increase the uses of self-assessment and peer-assessment, which depend far less on subjectivity of assessors, and allow far greater amounts of feedback to contribute towards successful learning experiences.
- provide training in assessing. Usually, a new lecturer is simply thrown in at the deep end. Participating with colleagues in a series of workshops on assessment-design can be much less intimidating, and allows discussion and feedback from experienced assessors.

9   *'If you can't measure it, it doesn't exist. If you can measure it, it isn't it'. What should we be trying to measure?*

It has been said that one of the main faults of our education and training systems is that we tend to teach people things that are already understood, instead of equipping them to understand new things. Assessment reflects this.

Suggestions:

- use self- and peer-assessment as an inherent part of *learning* processes, with the emphasis on learning rather than assessment outcomes.
- increase the use of a portfolio-approach to assessment. A balanced portfolio represents much more than the relatively trivial ability to answer examination questions against the clock.

10   *Where stops the buck? Whose fault is it that assessment is so artificial? Heads of Department? Employers? Assessors? Validators? The Government? Yours? Mine?*

If you imply that there is something suspect about people's abilities to assess, it is badly received! Assessment is something that is usually done privately rather than publicly and people go to great lengths to ensure that they retain privacy. Is such privacy really needed mainly because of the 'put down the number you first thought of' syndrome?

Suggestions:

- be brave - be prepared to experiment with new ways of assessing your learners - particularly when these involve learners themselves getting to know how assessment works.
- remember that there is much you can do without anyone else casting critical eyes over it. Traditional assessing is normally a rather private activity - take advantage of the privacy to try non-traditional ways of assessing.

Learning through assessing

In much of my discussion so far, I've been focusing on the dangers when assessment is 'done to' people, and hinting at the benefits which can result when learners themselves are allowed to be intimately involved in their own - and each other's - assessment.

Self-assessment and peer-assessment may lack some of the precision of the best of 'formal' assessment - where (some) assessors have a great deal of experience and (sometimes) assess fairly and conscientiously. However, what may be lacked in terms of precision is more than compensated for by the benefits of deeper learning, which go hand in hand with the act of learners themselves assessing.

Close encounters with assessment criteria

This is the crucial difference between formal assessment and self-assessment or peer-assessment. Learners find out a lot about any subject simply by applying assessment criteria to examples of work in that subject (whether the examples are self-generated, made by other learners or issued by a teacher). Previously, assessment criteria have seemed to learners to be the property of examiners. There has been a tendency for teachers to regard assessment criteria as quite private.

For many years, I marked O-level and A-level scripts for two of England's public examinations boards. The marking schemes were invariably labelled 'Secret' and sometimes I had to sign a declaration to the effect that after the marking was completed I would destroy all information relating to the marking scheme.

In Higher Education, it is usual to have some sort of external moderation of assessment, usually involving sending draft examination papers to lecturers in other institutions for feedback or approval. Even where model answers and marking schemes have been required to be sent to external examiners or moderators, the vital information in such schemes has seldom been shared with learners, and until relatively recently hardly ever *applied* by learners themselves. Yet when learners have the chance to get their hands on assessment criteria, they seem to develop a thirst for the information they can derive from them - leading to much deeper learning.

Self-Assessment and peer-assessment are not just self-testing

These forms of assessment when well-developed involve several processes:

- involving learners in identifying standards or criteria to apply to their work
- agreeing with learners the relative importance of different criteria, by developing a suitable scale of 'weightings'
- allowing learners to make judgments about the extent to which they have met these standards and criteria
- providing the opportunity for learners to discuss with each other (and with their tutors) matters arising from their assessment of their own work or each other's work
- facilitating discussion of the fairness and objectivity of the assessment

In other words, self-assessment and peer-assessment have a tangible learning payoff, not least that associated with the quantity and quality of feedback which learners gain about their own performances and (in peer assessment) about each other's performances.

Assessment criteria: black and white or shades of grey?

In subjects like maths, science and engineering, things are often either right or wrong - and it is relatively easy to devise assessment criteria for tests and exercises. However, even in subjects such as law or social studies, there are identifiable *hallmarks* of a good answer or an unsatisfactory answer to a question. Such hallmarks can be turned into checklists of a flexible kind, which enable the characteristics of good and less-good answers to be compared and contrasted. Students can benefit by learning in the act of applying assessment criteria to their own and each others' work.

Benefits to learners of close encounters with assessment criteria

Learners can quickly find out about incorrect assumptions they have been making. They are able to find out more and more detail about the answer to the crucial question: 'What am I expected to become able to do?'

There are, of course, many more benefits, depending on *how* we involve learners in using assessment criteria - including helping learners themselves formulate the criteria (when this is possible or appropriate) - leading to the most obvious form of ownership of assessment.

Some examples of self- and peer-assessment mechanisms

Self assessment is not confined to the variety that is widely used in open and distance learning (though of course that is one powerful form of it). Self- and peer-assessment processes can include any of the following:

- providing learners with assessment criteria devised by tutors, a marking scheme and allowing them to mark their own work
- as above, but then allowing learners the chance to compare *their* mark with that of a 'professional' marker
- as above, but *also* giving learners feedback about the *quality* of their self-assessment
- enabling individual learners to generate assessment criteria and use them to assess their own work
- enabling a group of learners to generate assessment criteria, and so on
- allowing learners to use *core* criteria generated by a group, plus *additional* criteria specific to their own pieces of work, with an agreed weighting
- groups of learners can be issued with criteria to apply to each others' work
- groups of learners could *produce* criteria and apply them to each others' work

There are further combinations of these. There is also the additional matter of whether the grades or scores contribute in a formal way to the performance records of learners.

Facilitating learners' ownership of assessment criteria

Where it is possible to draw assessment criteria from learners themselves, especially in group situations, the sense of ownership which learners develop is very powerful, and leads to them using the criteria with considerable enthusiasm and commitment when self- or peer-assessing. It is of course important to explain to learners the benefits they can draw from taking part in assessing their own or each other's work before proceeding further.

I have found that the following approach gives useful results for groups of 10-20. I have spelled out the process in some detail below, but you will often be able to take short cuts and simplify the task in the light of your own experience. Nonetheless, I have found that the whole of the sequence below can be completed in less than an hour with groups of around 25 learners.

Quality of assessment

Suppose learners are about to do task 'x' (where 'x' could be to write an essay, give a presentation, prepare a project, write a report, design a handout, and so on). After a general introduction to clarify the nature of the task, the time available and the general format of the final product, proceed as follows.

1. Ask each learner to *privately* list (e.g.) six things you would expect of a good 'x'
2. Ask learners to go into groups of 3 or 4 and discuss the criteria they have devised.
3. Encourage the groups to 'refine' the criteria, by (for example) turning them into checklist questions, and avoiding 'subjective' words such as 'interesting' or 'scholarly'.
4. Ask the *groups* to make a list of the most important of the criteria and to *prioritise* them.
5. Make a flipchart of criteria, starting by asking for the most important criterion from each group in turn, then the next most important, and so on. Naturally, expect overlaps and duplication among the criteria from different groups, and cluster them together as well as possible on the flipchart, or combine overlapping criteria while building up the list.
6. Ask the whole group whether anything important is missing from the flipchart list. There will usually be some further criteria worth adding at this stage, or some further adjustments to be made to the list.
7. Tidy up the flipcharted items if necessary, or even edit the list onto a new flipchart, and then number the criteria, e.g. 1-8
8. Ask each learner to privately distribute (e.g. 30) 'marks' among the criteria.
9. Where the group size is 30 or less, ask each of the learners in turn to speak out the score they allocated to 'criterion 1', writing the scores beside the criterion on the flipchart. Then do the same with 'criterion 2' and so on.
10. Normally, it is very clear which of the criteria are the most important ones from the scores allotted to them by most of the learners. Also, there may be one or more criteria attracting very low scores and it is often worth deleting these altogether.
11. Either average the scores out, or allow each of the learners to apply their own weightings in the peer-assessments to follow.
12. Brief the learners then go off to prepare to perform the task to be assessed (individuals or groups)
13. Produce and copy a grid with *their* criteria and weightings listed on it, ready for peer-assessment. (See Fig. 4 for a typical grid structure).
14. All learners then enter scores onto their copies of the grid, relating to each of the successive 'performances' (e.g. presentations or multiple-assessments of photocopied written work). It is particularly useful to additionally allow learners to enter scores self-assessing their own performances, allowing them in due course to compare their self-assessment with that given by their peers.
15. The grids can be signed by learners, or handed in anonymously and average scores can be computed for each of the overall performances - and for each of the criteria too if it is wished.

Quality of assessment

Peer Assessment Grid

Criteria	Weight	A	B	C	D	E	F	G	H
1									
2									
3									
4									
5									
6									
7									
8									
Total									

Figure 4 *Peer assessment grid*

An example

I helped a group of students from a Foundation Course in Science, Engineering and Technology to generate and prioritise some simple criteria for a short presentation that each student was to give to the group. (The presentations were optional; the assessment for the 'Learning Strategies' module of the course contained six equal elements and students could choose which five they tried - in other words they could choose *not* to give a presentation if they really wished to opt out.) We agreed that anyone who had the courage to get up and start immediately deserved to 'pass' - in other words they got the first 40 marks there and then. Seven criteria were then devised by the students to account for the remaining 60 marks, and the peer-assessment grids became as shown in Figure 5.

Quality of assessment

Peer Assessment Grid

Criteria	Weight	A	B	C	D	E	F	G	H
1 confidence	5								
2 staying on topic	5								
3 well illustrated	10								
4 well researched	10								
5 handouts overheads	10								
6 dealing with questions	10								
7 timing	10								
8 starting	40								
Total	100								

Figure 5. *Peer assessment grid for presentations*

Each student filled in a grid for each of the presentations he or she witnessed (and students additionally self-assessed their own using the same criteria). For various reasons, some students were only able to be present for half of the time involved and one or two students participated as assessors, but did not wish to give presentations themselves. I myself worked as one of the assessors and was relieved to find that, in general, the marks I awarded each of the presentations were close to the average mark for that presentation.

The raw data are presented in Table 1.

SETFY Presentations: 2 December: 1300-1700

	A	B	C	D	E	F	G	H	I	J	K	L	M	N	O	P	Q	average	title
Rhodri Woodcock	65	88	96	88	86	87		99		88	75	90	73	79	81	88	90	63	AIDS
Phil Race	67	82	75	79	88	89	73	95	71	80	66	79	72	66	79	73	75		(facilitator)
Brigene Baker	67	67	79	75		78	59	97		82	70	77	81	75	72	77	72	75	A German village
Kevin Ball	77	86	84	87	86	93	68	94	86	91	77	74	78	79	85	74	81	75	Playing the guitar
Alistair Powell	67	71	80	71	68	86	64	84										77	Playing the saxophone
Nick Jay	74	70	77	79	72	78	65	88	72	80	72	77	82	69	83	78	79		(non-presenter)
Sajid Ali	70	79	85	85	79	80	70	79											(non-presenter)
Khalid Haque	53	76	80	80	90	75	73	95		82	72	88	72	59	72	66	67	76	Arranged marriages
Paul Bartley	73	83	79	80	81	86	78	91	84	81	80	87	86	78	86	79	79	74	Home winemaking
Matthew Radford	71	76	77	78	85	78	67	72		80	70	86	77	79	67	78	72	71	Europe by rail
Anthony Lawton	61	67	66	64	69	69	61	67	65	71	62	75	70	65	67	66	70		(non-presenter)
Robert Owen	58	71	73	75	63	68	44	69	63	64	60	58	66	64	65	63	52	76	Rise and fall of Wales
Julian Williams	68	74	74	72	75	77	62	81	65	83	68	72	71	69	70	64	65	72	Dungeons and dragons
Darren Clarke	63	70	71	66	71	72	58	76	59	72	64	68	70	64	69	64	66	77	A trip to India
Huw Vaughan-Davies	67	75	76	80	80	83	67	90	73	72	64	64	69	80	76	68		67	Giving presentations
Martyn Bunn	65	77	65	75	73	78	56	68	74	70	64	73	66	64	65	63		83	Teaching swimming
Steven Thomas	66	70	76	74	72	79	61	79	68	78	76	71	77	65	68	65	65	70	Surfing
Ella Foster Aileru	64	62	59	68	60	58		60	64		62	63	62	63	60	57		69	Mountaineering club
Lika Abdulah	60	67	63	70	68	64	50	70	69	76	61	68	66	64	63	56	78	70	The Gulf crisis
Al-Mandhari	72	82			84	88	83	88		82	79	86	77	77	80	77		69	A Review of 1991
Justin Williams	67	75	72	78	85	67	52	78	69	78	58	76	75	67	64	51	60	78	Drinking games

Table 1. *Peer assessment data*

Allowing for individual differences

The sort of peer-assessment described above is suitable for tasks such as presentations, where many people can assess the same piece of evidence, and where scores can then be compared and discussed by the group. For individual tasks such as essays, reports, projects, dissertations and so on, it is likely that each piece of work will reflect slightly different criteria (or even *very* different criteria) and then is is often best to allow for some 'agreed' criteria, and some 'idiosyncratic' criteria so that each learner can exercise more ownership of the assessment criteria. An example of a grid that can be adapted for such purposes is shown in Fig.6.

Self Assessment Grid

Agreed Criteria	weight	score	Comments
Idiosyncratic Criteria			
Total			

Figure 6. *Self assessment grid*

The most important outcome of involving learners in the formulation of self-assessment or peer-assessment criteria is that learners address the task with criteria in their minds and the quality of their work seems to be much higher than it may otherwise have been. In other words, there is no longer the 'hidden agenda' of the criteria in the mind of the assessor. Instead, when learners use self-assessment and peer-assessment, they are already in possession of the 'rules of the game' and will strive particularly hard to live up to these rules, particularly when they have helped to make them in the first place. Furthermore, being involved in devising and applying assessment criteria gives learners a useful insight into how other parts of their work (for example, formal examinations) are likely to be assessed, and helps them to work out more about the 'rules' (or 'wiles'?) of exam marking too.

Throw away the numbers or grades?

I've often suggested to learners after a peer assessment exercise that the numbers or grades they awarded (if not contributing to their overall assessment) were only a *vehicle* to help them do learning of a higher productivity. However, I've found they usually want to hang on to the numbers - good or bad. Perhaps this is evidence of the sort of ownership we're aiming for?

How well can students assess themselves, and each other?

In general, students are quite accurate in their assessing. I have found that when students are asked to 'guess' their own performance scores just after completing an exam, around 90% of students 'guess' within 5% of their actual scores. It is useful to identify the 10% who had an inaccurate perception of how they had done - they usually benefit from a discussion to probe the causes. Those 10% may be over-anxious and underestimate their achievements, or over-confident and over-estimate their achievements. When discrepancies in self-assessment occur, they are usually due to one of the following causes:

- there is some tendency for learners to over-rate themselves in areas to which they are new; this tends to happen with the weaker members of a group.
- there is a tendency for some learners to under-rate themselves in areas in which they are experienced; this tends to happen with the more-skilled members of the group.

Peer-assessment and self-assessment can be usefully combined. Peer-assessment can be conducted 'blind' so that 'arranged' scoring is avoided. If the peer-assessment mark or grade is equal to the corresponding self-assessment mark (e.g. within 5%) then the self-assessment marks go forward into the assessment system - possibly with a staff 'scan' to ensure that fair play is in operation. (It is far quicker to *scan* a piece of work to check whether the assessment is fair, than it is to *mark* the work from scratch). When self- and peer-scores differ, negotiation or staff intervention may be necessary (but this happens surprisingly rarely in practice).

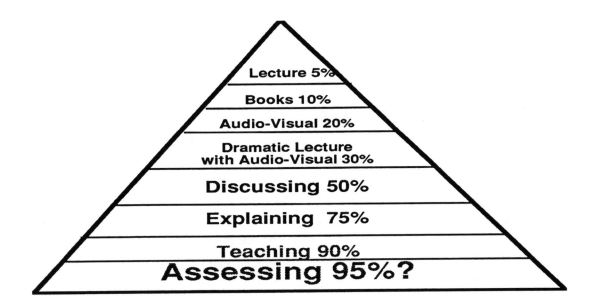

But can't it all go wrong?

There are several things that can go wrong with self-assessment and peer-assessment and to use either process successfully, it's worth knowing the potential dangers.

'You're paid to assess me - why should I assess myself?'

There will always be some learners who regard self-assessment or peer-assessment as an abdication from duty by tutors. My own reply is along the lines 'Certainly, I'll assess your work if you wish. But the real aim of involving you in assessing is not to save me work, but to allow you to gain much greater understanding not only of your subject material, but also of how assessment works'.

'But we haven't the expert knowledge to use to assess'

This, of course, is a real concern of many students faced for the first time with the task of assessing their own - or their colleagues - work. Tutors are regarded as 'expert witnesses' blessed with the experience with which to make authoritative and valid judgments. The key to solving problems of this nature is clarification of assessment criteria. When the criteria are phrased in language that learners can readily understand, their reservations about being able to make judgments based on the criteria are rapidly dispelled. In addition, with peer assessment, it is wise to spell out the advantages of a multiple judgment rather than the single one that might be given by a tutor. The average of several people's opinions is always likely to be more meaningful than a single opinion - even when the single opinion comes from a 'figure of authority' ie a tutor.

'What about passengers in team work?'

Often, when the products of team work are being self- or peer-assessed, the matter of 'contribution' comes up. One way is to award a score or grade to the overall product of the work of the team, whether it is a presentation, a report, an exhibition, or so on. Then, the team can be asked to 'split' the overall score between its members, in terms of the contribution each member made to the final product. Obviously, it's best if this can be done 'publicly' with all team members reaching agreement about the split of the award. Alternatively, however, it can be done by 'secret ballot', with the possibility of tutor intervention if necessary. Surprisingly perhaps, it is seldom necessary to invoke such extremes, especially if the issue of 'passengers' has been addressed by the whole group in advance and some groundrules on 'contribution' drawn up with the approval (better still, ownership) of the group as a whole.

'Is it the novelty that makes it work?'

Usually at present, when self-assessment or peer-assessment are introduced into a course, they have 'novelty value'. Because they are different, students tend to take them seriously and engage fully in the right spirit with their increased responsibilities. If such methods of assessment become commonplace, they would be regarded as part of the normal system, and human nature dictates that students would seek ways of 'playing the system' as in many other aspects of life. So, to some extent, it has to be admitted that the genuine enthusiasm and objectivity that students display for well-arranged self-assessment or peer-assessment has something to do with the novelty-value.

'What if the group just does not gel?'

Especially when assessing the product of group-work, there is always the possibility of a particular group having problems, possibly due to a single member. One way round this is to allow new groups to be formed for successive tasks, so that the effect of any disruptive or uncooperative individual is spread rather than concentrated. However, this can lead to what a colleague of mine referred to as 'sieving' of students, ending with the weakest all being left in a single group.

'But won't students be far too kind to themselves when they self-assess?'

Tutors are genuinely concerned, sometimes, that left to their own devices, students will all award themselves first-rate scores or grades. However, it is often the case that students' assessments are 'harder' than staff assessments. Admittedly, there are a few students who will self-assess their own efforts unrealistically 'high', but such instances are rare, and stand out clearly. If we are honest about it, students are in a better position to self-assess their own efforts than anyone else is. Even if they rate themselves too high, they almost certainly know they are doing just that. The real payoff is in the reflection that they engage in when making their judgments about their own work, whether rightly or wrongly. In other words, self-assessment is not a means to an end, but an end to a means - ie a way of helping students to reflect deeply. In the model of learning I use throughout this book, self-assessment is a very useful process which aids 'digesting'.

The discussion above shows that self-assessment and peer-assessment can certainly 'go wrong'. If either process is introduced by tutors who do not believe in the benefits that can be achieved, or to learners who are reluctant to engage fully with the processes, it is not hard to see how either process will be doomed to failure. It is important not to 'impose' innovations such as self- or peer-assessment against the will of tutors. Tutors are highly intelligent professionals and if forced to do something they don't trust will ensure that it demonstrably fails to work!

Self-Assessment, Peer-Assessment and how people learn

Throughout this chapter, I've advocated the benefits of helping learners become intimately involved in processes of assessing and I've pointed to the hazards of traditional assessment procedures. To conclude, let's look once again at the four main processes of learning I introduced in Chapter 1 and mentioned briefly earlier in this chapter and see how the processes of self- and peer-assessment relate to how people learn.

- *wanting* to learn (motivation)

  Motivation can be improved by early success. Self-assessment in particular can be used with the comfort of privacy and learners can gain confidence by finding that they are 'doing alright' long before they need to prove so publicly or formally. Also, motivation is greatly increased by 'knowing the rules of the game' of assessment. Self-assessment and peer-assessment take away many of the 'fear of the unknown' feelings about assessment.

- **learning by *doing* (practice, learning from mistakes, and so on)**
  There's no better way to find out about one's successes and failures than by finding them out for oneself in the comfort of privacy - or having a peer help one do this, rather than an 'authority figure' like a tutor or examiner. The very act of assessing is intrinsically 'learning by doing' - it involves the application of criteria, decision-making, judgment, and reflection. In other words, assessing is a 'deep' activity rather than a 'surface' one and avoids the passivity which can pervade many less-active forms of learning.

- **learning through *feedback* (to develop positive *feelings* about the learning)**
  The 'showstopper' of formal assessment has to be the dreadfully limited feedback that is the norm - ie just receiving a number or a grade. Peer-assessment can allow for a great deal of feedback - far more than could ever be given by a tutor or assessor (especially when class sizes are increasing). In addition, the feedback gained in peer-assessment is usually far less threatening than that from 'professional' assessors. It is therefore received in a more-relaxed way, without the heightened emotions often involved in receiving feedback from a figure of authority. Indeed, peers will often argue and debate issues, further deepening the usefulness of the feedback exchanges they receive.

- ***digesting* (taking stock, making sense of the experience, and of the feedback)**
  Both self-assessment and peer-assessment can help learners make sense of their learning experiences - and of the feedback they gain. Furthermore, the time lag between the learning and the feedback can be much less than with traditional methods of assessment. Therefore, the feedback is much more actively received and the learning thereby enhanced.

Reflecting on assessment

It can be argued that people who need a 'tester' are inadequately prepared to be sent out into the world outside. Self-assessment and peer-assessment can both be important parts of the learning process. The learning experience resulting from such forms of assessment is more important than the result of the assessment. Self-assessment or peer-assessment do not necessarily have to lead to any 'formal' (recorded) assessment. The aim can be purely as a learning experience, with the 'marks' simply part of the process through which that experience is facilitated.

Self-assessment and peer-assessment are skills, and become more reliable with practice. Receiving feedback on the quality of these forms of assessment is vital if learners are to derive the maximum benefit from engaging in them. Self-assessment and peer-assessment should be introduced early - for example during the first term rather than being left till the final year. Late in a course students may see little point in embracing new ways of learning.

'Ownership' is the most crucial aspect of successful learning and both self-assessment and peer-assessment are closely connected to the development of ownership of learning.

Not all students warm to the 'exposure' of self- or peer-assessment. They may begin their studies with expectations that they will be assessed by professionals. 'What's in it for me?' they naturally may ask. They need to be convinced that self- and peer-assessment have direct benefits for themselves, and do not represent an abdication from duties on the part of tutors. Some tutors, however, feel it is dangerous to 'lose control' of assessment. If such tutors try to employ self- or peer-assessment, but constantly safeguard their right to step in 'should things go wrong', the whole concept of such forms of assessment is undermined.

So what about teaching? Admittedly, our students learn from us. But they probably learn *more* on their own, and they probably learn *even more* from each other. Much of their learning occurs in the immediate run-up to assessment of one kind or another - so the role of assessment is an important factor in the *circumstances which accelerate learning*. Therefore, perhaps our biggest contribution to our students' learning is directly associated with the quality of the assessment our students encounter - and has less than we'd like to think to do with our teaching activities. I believe there is a strong case for using self- and peer-assessment not primarily to assess, but as processes to enhance learning.

Finally, if and when we must resort to traditional, formal assessment, I believe that there is a great deal of room for improvement. The 'ten worries' I expressed at the beginning of this chapter may help to set an agenda for improving the quality of assessment. I end this chapter with ten recommendations.

What can we do to improve assessment?

1 Extend and develop the competence-assessment approach, where people accumulate *evidence* of the things they do, and when they're ready, bring the evidence forward for assessment.

2 Use assessment as a learning opportunity. Give people feedback on their performance, and help to improve it. Make the primary purpose of assessment that of helping people find out how their learning is going, so that they can adjust their strategies accordingly.

3 Use assessing as a learning process - help learners to self-assess their own work and peer-assess their colleagues' work (whether or not the marks or grades are to 'count'). Let learners gain familiarity with the nature of the assessment criteria which they need to live up to. Help them find out what sort of performance they need to be able to give.

4 Change the culture where any professional can sit down and scribble down an exam question in a few minutes, to a culture where all important exams are made up entirely of questions which have been piloted, tested, evaluated and proved to measure desirable things.

5 Where learners need to take traditional assessment forms such as written examinations, build-in to their courses detailed advice on how best to prepare for exams, and how to tackle the task of giving written answers against the clock.

6 Develop team approaches to question setting and marking. Introduce at the very least double-marking as a standard for exams - and when possible multiple-marking.

7 Move away from the type of exams which mainly measure recall. For example, move towards open book exams, where learners' ability to 'make sense of information and apply it' can be tested.

8 Develop external moderation of assessment much further, for example by paying external examiners to 'blind-mark' a selection of examination scripts and compare marks with the internal assessors.

9   Pay people well for assessing, instead of just paying them for teaching. Teachers often earn 'holiday money' by doing extra exam-marking. It's all the wrong way round! Assessment is so important that perhaps it should be that assessors can earn 'holiday money' by doing a little teaching! Then require them to continuously demonstrate their competence at the job of assessing.

10   Take the results of traditional assessment less seriously, especially when selecting candidates for jobs. There are countless tales of 'well-qualified' people turning out to be entirely unsuitable for the real world of employment, yet almost every application form devotes a lot of space for educational records.

Reference

Saunders D and Race P (1992) (eds) *Developing and Measuring Competence: Aspects of Educational and Training Technology XXV* Kogan Page, London.

Chapter 5

BS5750 for assessment

Based on a report of a workshop which I led at the AETT 1992 Annual Conference at the University of York on April 7 1992.

Participants

J Arter, A F Bickerton, Brian Canniford, Chu-Poon Yap Ching, Julie Clerk, Paul Ellis, Chahid Fourali, J Greenacre, Rachel Hudson, Steve Leary, Peter Leckstein, Jill Lloyd, Patricia McCarron, Chris O'Hagan, Jack Oakley, Michael Owen, Larry Roberts, Bob Sayer, Michael Shoolbred, Prof A R Sykes, Christine Tan.

Abstract

This workshop report is an attempt to capture the experience of a diverse group of professional people, which was the greatest resource at this workshop. The following transcripts and analyses of things they did during the workshop should provide a basis for many improvements in the ways we use assessment processes and devices. The following Abstract had been published in the Conference documentation: 'The workshop will be a participative event, sharing the good (and bad) experiences of participants - both of assessing - and of being assessed. The workshop will begin by extending 'ten worries about assessment' (presented in Chapter 4 of this book). Syndicates will examine ways and means for overcoming the problems. The primary aim of the workshop is to generate a set of 'quality' criteria which can be applied to assessment processes, practices and instruments, to guarantee learners a fair and just assessment'.

Workshop aims and objectives:

- to pinpoint the weaknesses in assessment practices and devices
- to explore alternative ways of assessing
- to enhance the learning which can be derived from assessment
- to produce 'quality criteria' for assessment.

Participants' expectations

Participants were given a small piece of acetate and asked to write on it their answers to the question : *'what do you personally hope to gain from this workshop?'*. This allowed the workshop to address particular issues which participants had brought to the workshop. The acetates were displayed to the group and clarification encouraged where needed. Their expectations were as follows:

- Where assessment fits into BS5750.

BS5750 for assessment

- To get an idea of how BS5750 compares with other possible models.
- To use BS5750 creatively.
- To highlight quality criteria.
- Relating BS5750 to assessment, specifically quality manual documentation.
- How to improve assessment - ideas, experiences of others.
- When and how it can go wrong.
- Further ammunition and ideas for reforming assessment.
- Rationale for justifying democratic versus traditional assessment for use in the context of a traditional organisation.
- Identifying appropriate means of assessing (non-teaching background).
- Criteria for designing quality assessment; ideas on using computers for continuous assessment.
- Ideas to help colleagues to more effective assessment with less quantity of work (Exam board activity can surely be just as effective with fewer numbers to crunch!)
- Why BS5750 is in the title but not mentioned in the Abstract
- Clear ideas about quality assessment; how to avoid unhelpful assessment of students' work.
- New insights into the use of assessment .
- Changing students' expectations to accept student-centred assessment.
- How far should courses be 'assessment driven'? The relationship between assessment and outcomes. How far should the teaching and learning strategy reflect the assessment strategy?
- Ideas.
- Ideas to use in a course I am designing where I might be able to include diagnosis as a form of student learning.
- Some ideas on BS5750 criteria for assessment.
- Ideas, concepts to be of use in dealing with an awkward group of FE colleagues wrestling with problems of assessment.
- Find out a little about how FE/HE have initiated changes/improvements in assessment procedures, and how this is linked to 5750.

These expectations are of considerable interest in their own right. They illustrate the many different ways that people view assessment, and issues associated with assessment. Several expectations mentioned BS5750 in particular. At the start of the workshop, I 'came clean' at once on this, and indicated that the purpose of the workshop was to generate information which would lead to criteria for high quality in assessment, rather than to look at how existing BS5750 documentation may lend itself to applications to assessment.

Fitness for purpose
Participants were divided into syndicates and briefed as follows to consider particular types of assessment and prepare an overhead transparency addressing each of the following issues:

BS5750 for assessment

SYNDICATE TASK 1
Choose a type of assessment

- decide exactly what it actually assesses best
- discuss how it helps the processes of **learning**
- list some advantages and disadvantages of the type of assessment

The following are transcripts of the acetates produced by the syndicates and add up to an interesting exploration of a number of different possible processes of assessment.

1   Role Playing

What?	**Attitudes**	
	Procedural behaviour	
	Skills	(interpersonal)
		(problem solving)
		(self awareness)
	Applying theory	
How it helps	**Confidence boosting**	
	Practice	
	Experiential learning (remembered)	
	Time effective	

Advantages	Problems
Build a profile	Student reluctance
Guide to competence	'Ego trip' for some
Peer learning	Not taken seriously
Effective learning	Unreal
Instant feedback	Traumatic, subjective

2   Oral Presentation on behalf of a group
What it assesses

Group Work	Individual
Content against objectives	presentation style
Design and organisation	voice
Time management	use of audio-visual aids
Visual aids	
Use of sources	
Ability to answer questions	

How it helps learning
- Immediate feedback
- Group learning
- Peer tutoring
- Peer assessment

Advantages	Problems
validity	time consuming
good learning environment	free riders
	design consistency

BS5750 for assessment

3   Self-assessment

What it assesses
An example: bricklayers and total quality management programme

How it helps Learning

- ownership
- involvement

Advantages	Disadvantages
Involvement leads to motivation	How will they judge for themselves their ability to implement their learning?
Realisation of responsibility	Cost of establishing competence criteria
Focuses responsibility	Being adhered to?
Another ethic throughout the organisation	Policing outcomes
	Abdication of responsibility?
	Honesty? Cover up mistakes?

4   Student Self-Assessment
Examples: portfolio of work, exhibitions microteaching, teaching a lesson

What it assesses

- students perceptions of their own learning
- **all areas** (Bloom)

How it helps learning

- leads to learner autonomy

Advantages	Disadvantages
reflective	abuse?
diagnostic	subjectivity
developmental	false humility
load taken from tutor	subversive

5   Performance Assessment

What is assessed?
Conformity to norms: job-related criteria

How it helps learning

It can help learning, but it aims:

- to qualify
- to certify competence
- to verify

Advantages   **Disadvantages**

clarity   time to establish

a working tool

6 Skills Assessment

- skills being assessed
- conditions specified
- standards of achievement identified

What is assessed - ability to carry out task or perform skill
How it helps learning

- sequences/prioritises the learning process
- identifies difficulties

Advantages   **Disadvantages**

- indicates skills   • resource demands heavy
- 'I can do'   • resource driven
  - feel good factor

Individual recollections of assessment

Participants were issued with post-it slips, and asked several questions about the last assessment they themselves had experienced as learners.

Their replies are transcribed on the following pages. They show a fascinating range of feelings about assessment, attitudes towards the results of assessment, and views about what (if anything) was learned from the various experiences of being assessed.

It should be remembered, however, that the participants themselves represented learners who had succeeded. Their views would therefore be expected to be considerably more positive than an average group of learners, whose future careers may still depend upon what happens next time they are assessed.

Individual Task Briefing

Think back to the last time you were assessed.
On a post-it, write notes under the following headings:

A   What form did the assessment take?
B   How did you feel just before the assessment?
C   How do you now feel about that assessment?
D   What was assessed? Was it process, product or something else?
E   What did you learn from that assessment?

A Form of Assessment	B Feelings just before	C Feelings now	D. What was assessed	E. What was learned
1 day at assessment centre psychometric test, formal presentation, groupwork interviews	v. nervous anxious to perform well	It was efficient it aimed to be objective I feel good about it	Management style, flexibility, depth/range of learning experience	very little other than about an assessment process
Written essays	very tense	calmer now	process, product + something else	knowledgeable about the subject tested yet gaps in my knowledge
Demonstrating comm. skills	Nervous but confident	satisfied	process and product	
Interview	Nervous but also glad to have the opportunity to try to sell myself	Very pleased because the process gave me the chance to sell myself	Analytical abilities personal qualities	I confirmed that interviews are a process I quite enjoy.
End of year exam	Slightly tense but fairly confident; relieved	One should not be judged on the basis of one day's result	process and product (psychology course)	How to determine fair criteria for assessment

BS5750 for assessment

A Form of Assessment	B Feelings just before	C Feelings now	D What was assessed	E What was learned
Reading, writing, interview using English and French	Surprised	Reassured by useful nature of assessment	Process: reading French listening to French, summarising, thru product writing in English	The need to improve my listening skills, mostly.
PhD Oral examination	v. apprehensive about the nature of the dialogue with the examiner (i.e. aggressive)	Good test that I had done the work and understood it and the background.	That the work was my own. Intellectual skills. Ability to summarise. Logical thought.	Nothing much but that wasn't the point (or was it?)
Written/oral	No special feeling	No special feeling except my work is appreciated.	Skills of cooperation	One's energies were readily appreciated and accepted by one's boss.
Verbal grilling	Uneasy (no forewarning)	Good	Product and process - ability to rapidly assimilate data/info - formulate coherent answers - communicate answers	Beware! Better knowledge of how to handle this individual.
Open book exam (written)	Confident	Fine - I passed!	Process	That I have a good memory.
Written exam	Tense	Too much to study and memorise	Product	Can't remember!

BS5750 for assessment

A Form of Assessment	B Feelings just before	C Feelings now	D What was assessed	E What was learned
Assignment	Unsure as to the standard required.	It gave me a degree of autonomy in the learning process.	process/product required.	The standard of learning
Submitted papers	Inadequate - that I might not have sufficiently coherent story.	Choice of examiner might have been critical.	product	Nothing
Questionnaire to students about quality of a 10-week course.	Always vaguely anxious	Quite happy	Teaching performance Relevance and interest to students of material.	Course is basically OK so is my teaching (probably better than the material)
Oral questioning 'viva voce'	Terrified	Relieved, then depressed then elated	process, product: results and conclusions	How to do it better. checking out carefully.
Score, with written feedback making comments.	Apprehensive, excited. Hoping for good grade.	Good, as I obtained a high grade.	Content being process and product	I know more than I thought. Recognition of hard work.
Practical exam	Very anxious	angry	Conformity and sang froid	Not to bother taking it again. Incompetence of the examiner, both technically and as a person.
2-hour test	distraught	empty	my ability to write at speed.	That it did not test my understanding of the process.

BS5750 for assessment

A Form of Assessment	B Feelings just before	C Feelings now	D What was assessed	E What was learned
Unseen written test on profit/loss accounts.	Nervous, unhappy	Glad I was brave enough to abandon the course at that point.	Product. Stored knowledge regurgitated.	That I have no aptitude for financial management.
Written test	Tense	Nothing, long ago	Product	Nothing of importance.
Presenting audit findings in front of video (leading a panel)	Sick	Happy because it went well - passed.	Content of audit. Method of telling them.	Must be well prepared. Stick to facts, not opinions.

Notes

- The different types of assessment listed above show that in the 'real world' traditional forms of assessment (such as written exams) play a much smaller role than is often imagined.

- Most of the feelings just before the assessment (of whatever kind) are 'negative', and therefore are probably undermining the quality of the learning experience at that stage.

- The feelings 'after the event' tend to be mostly positive in the cases listed above. This is largely because the various assessments tended to be successful. With a 'normal' cross-section of people (i.e. *not* delegates at an International Conference), there tends to be considerably more 'anger' and 'frustration' when people reflect on the lack of appropriateness of various kinds of assessment that have been applied to them.

- 'What was assessed': the entries under this heading span a very wide range of skills and attributes. Only some of these can be attempted to be measured using conventional traditional assessment measures.

- 'What was learned' entries are very revealing. Often, the learning outcomes have little to do with the skills or knowledge being assessed. This demonstrates that the lack of detailed feedback in many assessment procedures is responsible for 'missed learning opportunities'.

'Laying down the law'

Participants were again divided into syndicates, and asked to produce an overhead transparency giving their recommendations for 'criteria for quality in Assessment'. Each syndicate presented its acetate briefly to the whole group. The following are transcripts of the acetates produced.

1	Recommendations for Assessment
1	Of both process and product
2	Emphasis on verification/certification of **product**

It must:
- be standardised - as a process
- give practical feedback
- be standardised against established criteria/objectives
- be valid /content/predictive
- be reliable
- be appropriate to the task
- be easy and practical to use

2   Laying down the laws:

(i)   Never use just one method to assess anything - use as many as possible.

(ii)   Avoid numbers (or letters) as 'marks' where possible. Use words.

(iii)   Be diagnostic where possible, not normative. (**Act** on the diagnosis).

(iv)   Be student-centred where possible (Profiles, not single shots).

(v)   Explain all criteria used **beforehand** to the students. If possible, negotiate them with the students.

(vi)   Spread the load on both students and staff.

(vii)   If judgmental, be gentle.

(viii)   Failure -> diagnosis -> counselling -> opportunity -> success.

3   Criteria for high quality assessment

- Exams scrapped!
- Honest
- Fast feedback
- Concise, no jargon
- Fair
- Encouraging, confidence-building
- Achievable

- Continuous
- Not threatening
- Learning experience
- Flexible

4   Criteria for Quality Assessment

(1)   Link assessment to outcomes of teaching - i.e. what did you plan for students to know, understand, and become able to do?

(2)   Use assessment to:

- identify what students may need to learn
- celebrate what students have achieved
- diagnose students' problems
- suggest how students can improve (formative)
- summarise what students know at the end of a course
- give information to future employers.

(3)   Use different assessment techniques to match different course approaches. Don't rely on one method of assessment.

5   Laying down the Law:
- Asking the right questions about assessment?

- Is it necessary?
- Is it relevant to the course objectives?
- Is it valid?
- Is it accurate and reliable?
- How does it build confidence?
- How does it lead to learning?
- How does it reinforce learning?
- Does the assessment drive the curriculum, or the curriculum drive the assessment?
- Is it fair to different students?
- Can the students practise?
- Can students know the criteria?
- Can students influence the criteria?
- Can quality feedback be given to students?
- Can the results of the assessment be used to redesign the assessment strategy and the teaching/learning strategy?

6   A Visual Approach

Below is a transcript of an overhead transparency prepared by one of the syndicates.

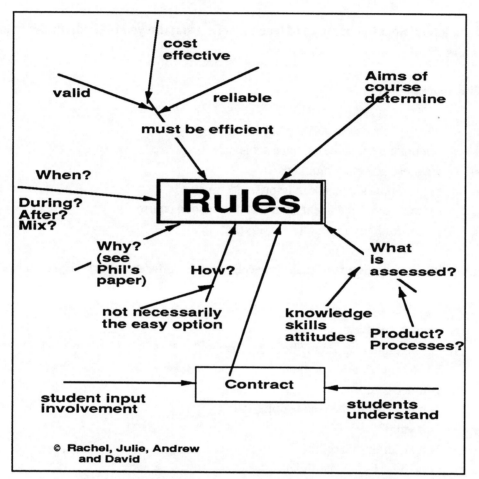

One Syndicates 'Laying down the Laws'

Conclusions

I had fun running this workshop, and I think participants rather enjoyed it as well! It was a 'busy' workshop; participants produced a great deal of material in the 90 minutes involved. Although delegates to an International Conference on Education and Training are somewhat self-selecting in that they are people whose education and training experiences tend to have been highly successful, I hope that this collection of their wisdom and experience may be useful in helping to make assessment processes in general better-suited to their purposes. I hope that in particular, we may move further towards using assessment as a valuable part of the learning process, rather than a way of measuring how far the horse may have bolted after leaving the stable door unlocked!

Chapter 6

Getting the assessment right

(Based on an article I published in 'Multimind' in September 1992)

Abstract

This chapter is an expanded version of a newsletter article, in which I expressed some of the concerns I introduced in Chapter 4. Unlike Chapter 4, however, this chapter is as much written to people who are going to be assessed as to those who are going to do the assessing. While at face value some of the views in this chapter may undermine learners' trust in assessment, the content of the chapter should be of some comfort to learners who have had bad experiences of being assessed - not least in that it shows them that in all probability much of the blame does not rest with themselves.

Getting credit for what you've learned

Learning is a natural human activity. It is often enjoyable. It is sometimes painful. It is seldom wasted. It is always an activity which leads to greater fulfilment and satisfaction. But what about assessment? If you've learned something, you *know* that you've done it. But for you to get credit for it, there has to be some demonstrable *evidence* that you've learned it successfully. That's where assessment comes in.

There are many different kinds of assessment. The most familiar is the traditional written examination. Examination results are used as the primary indicator of what people have learned. Examination results determine people's careers. Even when the exams were taken decades ago, every time you fill in an application form for a job, you're asked for a catalogue of your results. It does not seem to matter whether or not you've forgotten all of the material you once learned; those exam results still count.

Think about the education and training systems in operation throughout the world. The end-product of learning is always some form of assessment. So it could be argued that all the resources put into education and training are being channelled ultimately into one direction - that of *measuring* what people have learned. It is taken for granted that the processes of assessment are fair, accurate and reliable. ***They're not!***

Getting the assessment right

In this article, I would like to share with you my concerns about several aspects of the way we measure learning. My views are based on over twenty years of involvement with assessment. I've been an examiner for GCSE and 'A'-level exams. I've set and marked my own exam papers. I've prepared students for public examinations. I've moderated other people's exams and standards. I've been an 'external examiner'. Not least, I've taken a fair number of examinations in my time (and passed them all) - but am aware of what they measured, and what they failed to measure.

We're not good at it!

Anyone can buy a red pen. This does not mean that they can use it well when it comes to assessing exam papers (or essays, or projects, or dissertations, or reports). There have been countless experiments, where the same piece of work has been given to several different people to assess. In some cases, the 'mark' for the piece of work could range from 37% to 87%. Or the 'grade' could range from an A-minus to a D-plus. Yet at least 90% of the assessments that take place in schools, colleges and training centres are done by individuals, with no-one looking over their shoulder to check whether their assessment is objective or subjective.

It is taken as a 'divine right'

When people are employed as teachers, trainers, or lecturers, it is assumed that they have a God-given gift to assess people's work fairly. But think *why* they were appointed in the first place. Almost all appointments are made because of people's special knowledge or ability in a particular field. The history lecturer is appointed on the basis of scholarship in history. The maths teacher is good at maths. This does not mean that these people are automatically able to set good assessment tasks or to judge people's work with skill and precision. How many people who assess were appointed on the basis of their skills at assessing? Few.

Assessment is done in a rush by tired people

The vast majority of assessment is done 'in bulk'. I well remember the years when there would be a pile of scripts on my desk. Sometimes there would be hundreds. There would always be a deadline. The results would all be needed by a given date. The assessment may be measuring the learning accumulated over months or years, but the assessment itself is often given only a few minutes!

Assessment is usually done by bored people

After marking five hundred answers to the same question, I would be very tired of seeing the same sorts of answers - and particularly the same mistakes. Marking the scripts would become a real chore. Even if one was doing it fairly, it was only too easy to be thinking of all sorts of other things rather than the task in hand.

We don't ask the right questions!

After marking a pile of answers to a question, it is often possible to think of several improvements to the way the question had been worded. Different candidates would find different ways of interpreting the question. This would be reflected in their marks or grades. But there's something even more sinister than this. In our efforts to ask questions with minimum dangers of misinterpretation, we tend to ask *particular* questions which concentrate on that which it is relatively easy to measure. In other words, the assessment system militates against the sort of question which probes deep into a subject or which allows candidates to demonstrate their versatility and mastery in a variety of ways.

Assessment can be accurate, but still measure the wrong things

For many years I was a member of a team of thirty-odd examiners, all marking the same paper from schools throughout Britain. The chief examiner led the team well. He would design a very fair marking scheme for the paper each year, and the thirty-odd of us would gather for a morning and fine-tune the marking scheme into great shape. At the end of the process, we would all be able to mark any candidate's answer, and agree within 2%. So the assessment was demonstrably fair. Moreover, a third of the scripts were double marked to ensure that each member of the team was being fair (and if a 'suspect' examiner was discovered, *all* of his or her scripts would be re-marked). But despite all this accuracy, we knew we were still not really measuring whether candidates were good at the subject. All we could measure was whether they were good at answering the particular questions on the exam paper.

What do we actually measure?

When I'm conducting sessions on 'exam technique' for higher-education students, one of the overheads I show them poses a series of questions about exactly *what* is being measured. It goes without saying that a complex mixture of several of the things listed are involved in exam assessment - particularly 'how often you've practised answering exam questions'. (A copy of the overhead is included in Chapter 4 on page 46).

Candidates rarely know the rules of the game

The people who really know the rules of the game of assessment are the people wielding the red pens. Whether we're thinking of exam papers, reports, essays or dissertations - the rules of the assessment game seem to 'belong' to the assessors. Some assessors defend their right to keep these rules secret. They claim that if candidates knew what counted (and what lost marks) they would all-too-easily be able to prepare for assessment. Surely, that's a *good* reason for letting learners in on the rules of the game? Anything which helps learners to focus their learning is useful.

What about the things that can't be assessed?

Not everything lends itself to 'formal assessment'. Examples of things which can't be assessed directly include teamwork skills, interpersonal skills, leadership qualities, and lateral thinking. Assessment systems tend to ignore such things, and blindly go on measuring what people *know*, rather than trying to get a measure of what people *can do*.

Assessment fosters competition, not collaboration

This rather goes without saying! Exam rooms are very quiet places. People are prohibited from communicating with each other. Candidates usually even *prepare* for the ordeal with some secrecy. They don't want anyone to know how much they can do. The world outside, however, requires people who can work collaboratively, but the more people learn, the more competitive they are conditioned to become.

Assessing competence?

The term competence is increasingly favoured, as it implies not just what people know, but what they can do with it. However, many traditional kinds of assessment don't measure 'can do' skills, but only measure 'once did' reflections of some of those skills. Or in many cases, what is measured amounts to 'once did, on one's own, against the clock'. This amounts to a very distorted ghost of candidates' real competences.

Does assessment foster 'deep' learning?

We increasingly talk about the benefits of deep learning versus surface learning. Deep learning involves people gaining a real feeling of ownership of the skills and knowledge they acquire. Surface learning is simply a short term expedient, but is useful when the assessment system requires that candidates demonstrate 'did once' competences rather than 'is doing regularly, well' competences.

Assessment measures skills at choosing what not to do?

Many assessment systems give candidates choice. The choice may be any five out of eight questions in three hours. Or the choice may be over the topic of the report or essay. But what about all the things not chosen? Surely this becomes a licence to say 'I'll not bother with this'. In other words, our assessment systems are tending to measure people's skills at deciding what they're not going to learn - or their skills at deciding what they haven't learned successfully. These may indeed be useful skills, but not the main sort we should be encouraging.

Assessment is usually a lost learning opportunity

What *feedback* do people get after assessment? Often it's just a number or a grade. They rarely get the chance to see exactly what they did well - and more important - exactly what they did not do well. It's well known that one of the most productive ways of learning anything is from one's own mistakes - but how can people tell what mistakes they've made if we only give them scores or grades? Now if the *real* purpose of assessment was to give people feedback, assessment would be serving a useful role in the learning process (and scores and grades would cease to matter as much).

(The article concluded with some of the suggestions for improving assessment, now given at the end of Chapter 4).

Chapter 7

Appraising assessment
- The sharp end

Abstract

This chapter is built on the products of a workshop I led at the SCED Conference at what is now the University of Derby, on 21 May 1992. The published aims of the workshop were as follows:

- to share several worries about assessment - particularly formal assessment
- to explain why assessment may prove to be 'the sharp end' of appraisal
- to define some performance indicators for 'high-quality' assessment
- to define staff development needs in the area of assessment

The workshop abstract in the conference handbook was as follows.

'Casting aspersions at colleagues' assessment skills is more dangerous than implying that they may be deviant, criminal or insane. Yet the most important thing we do (from our students' point of view) is *assess*. The future careers of our students are more dependent on our skills at assessing than on our skills at teaching. Colleagues are quick to use the words 'professional judgment' when discussing how they assess. Despite claims to the contrary, there is evidence that 'putting down the number we first thought of' is far from extinct. Self-assessment and peer-assessment can provide ways of turning assessment into meaningful learning experiences (as opposed the the 'lost learning opportunities' which characterise most examinations).

The workshop will aim to tackle the situation head-on, by establishing a code of practice for high-quality assessment and will explore the staff development implications for making the quality of assessment (rather than of teaching or of research) centre-stage in higher education?

Summary of Workshop

Participants were each given a small piece of acetate and asked what their main expectations of the workshop were. They ranged from serious concerns about assessment, to those who simply come to my workshops for fun! I started the workshop by reviewing the 10 worries about assessment discussed in Chapter 4 and linking assessment to the model of learning introduced in Chapter 1, showing how traditional assessment methods were at cross-purposes with the ways in which most people learn. I then issued participants with Post-it slips, and asked for more worries and concerns about assessment. A wealth of ideas emerged and are transcribed in this report. In two syndicate activities, participants addressed 'recommendations for high-quality assessment' and the resulting 'recommendations for appraisal'. All the syndicates reported by quickly preparing overhead transparencies summarising their conclusions. The overheads are transcribed in this report.

My thanks are due to the following participants : Romla Hadrill, Margot Taylor, Gareth Owen Jones, Prof C S Williams, Dr Pat Cryer, Sandra Griffiths, Dr Alan Vincent, James Wisdom, W S Telfer, Arnold Goldman, C I Rust, Graeme Hill, Jenni Wallace, Sue Blything-Smith, Eric Revell.

Ten more worries about assessment - John Cowan and Phil Race

The following additional 'worries' about assessment grew out of correspondence with Dr John Cowan, Scottish Director of the Open University. I had earlier sent him a draft version of the '10 Worries' outlined in Chapter 4 and his rapid reply added many additional issues which should be regarded as cause for concern. At the present workshop, I displayed overheads both of my original ten 'worries' and the following ten.

11 There's often a mismatch between what's assessed and what the published syllabus indicates that we value. Many things on most syllabi don't ever get assessed and some of the things we do assess are relatively trivial.

12 Assessment tends to measure things in people's short term memories and they therefore adopt surface learning techniques to succeed. Assessment methods don't provide a driving force for 'deep learning'.

13 Assessment tends to be governed by examinations formats - for example 'five questions out of eight in three hours'. Therefore, all questions have to be answerable in half an hour, and need to be made equally difficult. This limits opportunities to ask 'hard' things as well as 'easier' things.

14 Most exams offer students a choice of questions. Success, therefore, depends substantially on students' decision-making skills under pressure - not the main thing we should be testing.

15 Almost all assessors hide from the fact that their assessing depends on mood, number of scripts already marked, subjective interpretation of questions and concepts, and many other factors. In short, assessing is usually unsound.

16 Although some research addresses compensation between examiners' standards (when a team of examiners is used), little research seems to address the unreliability between one examination and the next.

17   Students rarely get feedback showing exactly where they gained or lost marks, and why. Marking schemes and marked scripts are locked away after exams. As far as students are concerned, most exams are, therefore, lost learning opportunities.

18   Schemes of assessment encourage students to develop skills and attitudes contrary to many of those we value. Learning and assessment seem to be poles apart.

19   It is suspected that certain types of question disadvantage particular categories of students: for example: multiple choice questions (women?), eloquently worded questions (people learning in a second language?) longwinded questions (visually-minded people?).

20   Most assessment schemes depend on the culture of expectation of assessors. To what extent is poor performance caused by learners' failure to assimilate this culture (often because the culture is well-hidden), rather than a lack of competence?

I then issued post-it slips to participants to brainstorm in writing their additional concerns about the process and practices of assessment. The transcriptions of their concerns, given below, add considerably to the issues that need to be addressed if assessment is to be improved.

Participants' post-it worries and concerns

- Am I being fair? (ensuring that my view of the individual isn't affecting my marking of an assignment)
- Could the individual be more involved in the *process,* ie be a part of the assessment?
- Obsession with the normal curve of distribution; why shouldn't all the students be able to do well?
- The need to clarify and agree criteria for assessment with students.
- The need to use assessment as an integral part of the learning process and not as something different, or something alienated from the learning process.
- You've talked about the mood of the assessor; what about bias as well? Back to my original concern - the lack of training for assessors.
- Questions asked in final examinations of a magnitude - asking for a breadth of assimilation - not required in essays or discussed with students beforehand. Mismatch between exams and other performance opportunities.
- How do we overcome the absolute boredom on the part of assessors who are doing the same thing for years? How do we keep them stimulated?
- My worries are all focused on the issue: 'please, please direct resources to the training of management skills before we even consider appraisal training'.
- Using one method (i.e. exams) as if it measures all things (outcomes, competences, etc) equally or satisfactorily.
- Am I influenced by the legibility, spelling, grammar of the answers? Should these factors influence me? Am I consistent with my colleagues in this area?
- How do I mark a 'minimalist' effort by a student who I know from the course is very capable? Am I influenced by what I know about the knowledge of the student? If so, are all students treated equally?

- Breaking with tradition. How can it be demonstrated that new forms of assessment compare favourably with traditional forms? Is it possible to have controls?
- It is an over-riding responsibility of teachers (those with power through knowledge) to create opportunities for those they teach to grow, to succeed, to do well and to flourish. Assessment so often emphasises learners' failures, weaknesses, inabilities, insecurities, etc.
- The lack of agreed criteria between staff and students, or students not knowing what the criteria are.
- The need to ensure that we *are* assessing what we think we are assessing.
- Is it possible to assess more-objectively? (i.e. how can the subjective elements be reduced?)

Checklists of criteria for high-quality assessment

Participants at the workshop were grouped into syndicates and asked to formulate criteria for high-quality assessment. I have expanded and edited the products of the syndicate work, into the list of questions given below.

- Are the assessment criteria agreed with students? (ownership)
- Are all assessors using identical criteria for comparable assessment?
- Are the purposes of assessment clear to learners? (developmental, judgmental, or a mixture of both?)
- Is the choice of method of assessment appropriate for the learning objectives?
- Is feedback remaining as helpful and meaningful as it once was, as student numbers increase?
- Are all assessors giving an identical quality of feedback?
- **Are the assessors trained in assessment techniques?**
- Is the marking method appropriate to the learning outcomes?
- **Does the assessment design enable students to show their best, not probe for their worst?**
- Have the assessment methods been checked to ensure they achieve their purposes?
- Are the outcomes generally recognised and agreed?
- Is the assessment something that students will look forward to?
- Is there consistency between assessors?
- Is there a set rubric for assessment? (e.g. ignore handwriting, awareness of pitfalls)
- Are students fully aware of the criteria to be used? (also assessors).
- Does the assessment scheme eliminate subjectivity in assessment?
- Is the scheme designed so that criteria will be applied in same way by all assessors?
- Does the scheme use the most appropriate method for what's to be tested?
- Will the assessors believe in the assessment method?
- Does the scheme allow students to be counselled about their own performance?
- Is it integral? Who owns it?
- Does it further learning? Is it fair?
- Does it help to develop the student's own judgment?
- Is there some variety of mode? Choice of mode? (i.e. to what extent can we allow students to select the mode of assessment they participate in, or to what extent should all students 'compete on the same playing field'?)

- Do the instructions communicate clearly what students are to do, and to what standard?
- Does the scheme give appropriate choice?
- Does the scheme allow students to demonstrate knowledge, understanding, etc, using systems which do not suppress individuals?
- Is the assessment a process-based activity relevant to learning programmes, without introducing new terms, jargon, theories, etc.?

Recommendations for staff development and appraisal

The following recommendations for staff development and appraisal were produced by the workshop syndicates.

- Recommend to institutions that their appraisal schemes be developmental rather than solely judgmental; then:
  - check whether individuals have attended training in assessment;
  - check whether course teams have attended training in assessment as teams;
- Are all assessment techniques (e.g. self-assessment) used as appropriate?
- Are assessment techniques appropriate to acceptable staff workloads?
- Follow up students - performance in practice reflects the standing of assessment.
- Use external examiners to check:
  - the uniformity of marking
  - the appropriateness of criteria
  - consistency with other institutions.
- Obtain feedback from students and assessors on:
  - the appropriateness of assessment methods;
  - the fairness of the system.
- Ask staff the questions:
  - how does assessment in your teaching help further your students' learning?
  - how does each form of assessment relate to your course aims and objectives?
- Discuss statistical outcomes: pass rates, mark distributions, year to year comparisons, comparisons with other examiners. Ask for reasons for differences.
- Ask staff to present evidence of quality assessment criteria, ways that they share criteria with students, checking, relevance, etc.

Conclusions

The products of this workshop show that the concerns about assessment which I have included in this chapter (and the previous three) are widely shared by many people in education and training. Since assessment is such an important part of both education and training, it is crucial that it is well designed, well monitored, and above all that people involved as assessors are much better trained than has hitherto been commonplace. In designing schemes to estimate teaching quality, one of the most important factors to be measured is the performance of staff as they design and conduct assessments. The quality of assessment design should be a central issue in staff appraisal schemes. There needs to be a major and sustained staff development thrust designed at improving assessment policies and practices, for the various 'worries' about assessment raised in the last four chapters of this book to be resolved.

Chapter 8

Designing for open learning

Abstract

This is the first of two chapters in this book relating to open and flexible learning. The present chapter is intended to help teachers and trainers who are thinking about developing flexible learning materials of their own. Once again, my discussion of the design of open learning materials relates to the model of learning I introduced in Chapter 1. I leave to the following chapter a more extensive discussion of the meaning of open and flexible learning and the criteria for quality in learning resource materials.

How do people really learn?

In the last two thousand years or so, quite a lot has been written about how people learn. Indeed, people have been learning for some millions of years, and my guess is that while we have changed the nature of *what* we learn, we have not changed much regarding *how* we learn. In recent times, most of the theories of learning have been detailed and complex, written by psychologists, and it has become fashionable to use long words to describe learning. However, as you may have seen from Chapter 1, I've recently been advancing my own 'universal theory of learning' (in short words), based on the response of *real* people to questions about how they learn.

People are already 'open learners'

My first conclusion is that most of the learning people do is by what, nowadays, we call 'open learning' processes - in other words, at their own pace, in their own way and at times and places of their own choosing. So, designing open learning materials is simply a matter of designing materials from which people can learn in their own natural ways. However, there's a lot more to it than simply writing all the knowledge down - textbooks have been around for most of recorded history and we've all experienced how easy it is to spend hours with textbooks *without* any substantial learning payoff being derived from them. Learning resources need to contain much more than just information, and looking at *how* people learn is the best way to determine what needs to be added.

Linking open learning to how people learn

In Chapter 1, I introduced a model of learning which can be expressed in a few lines - there are four main stages as follows.

1   *Wanting to learn, and knowing what to learn, and why;*
2   *Learning by doing;*
3   *Learning from feedback;*
4   *Digesting what has been learned.*

In short, it's a sequence of wanting, doing, getting feedback and digesting. Each of these four natural stages in the learning process has implications in designing open learning materials. In this article, I'd like you to think about each of the four steps in turn and relate them to the components of open learning materials.

Creating the 'want' (- and responding to 'what?' and 'why?')

Motivation is a key foundation for successful learning, and in plain words motivation is about 'wanting'. It's no use just 'wanting' vaguely, however. People need to be able to see exactly what they can learn from an open learning package and why it will be useful to them. Several ingredients of an open learning package can be polished up, so that people are attracted towards it and stimulated to begin it.

- *The title*
  Titles can be attractive - or off-putting. Which would you choose from a selection of packages with the following titles?
  'Elements of Chemical Thermodynamics IV'
  'Getting to Grips with Thermodynamics'
  'Introductory Accountancy for Turf Accountants'
  'Balancing your Betting-shop Books'
  It helps, too, if the package *looks* interesting, with a stimulating and attractive cover design. After all, the title and cover also play a big part in helping people to *choose* a package in the first place.

- *Aims, objectives, competence statements*
  People (not surprisingly) want to know exactly what they will become able to do when they have worked through an open learning package. They need to be helped to *want* to achieve the objectives - and not to be frightened off by them. They need to see the relevance of the competences that the package will enable them to demonstrate.
  'When you've worked through this package, you'll be able to write a good short story' is a much more attractive objective than *'the expected learning outcome of this package is that the student will be able to compose a short work of creative fiction'* (at least, I think it is!).

- *The introduction*

  I'm always telling authors of open learning materials 'You never get a second chance to make a good first impression'. It's obvious really. That first paragraph or two sets the mood in which learners proceed. The first page or so should be written with a great deal of care (preferably *after* the whole of the rest of the package has been written, so that it can point firmly towards things to come).

- *But I know this already?*

  No-one comes to a new subject completely ignorant. Everyone knows *something* about a topic - even if it's just a series of questions they want to find out the answers to. In addition, people don't like to *feel* ignorant! Therefore, to help sustain the 'want', people need to be given credit for what they know already - it needs to be valued. One of the best ways of valuing what people already know is to give them the chance to tell you, then reply to them along the lines 'well done, you're absolutely right'. It's perfectly possible to do this in open learning materials, by setting early exercises which most people should be able to do correctly, and responding positively to what they do with the exercises. But, we're overlapping already into the second and third phases of my model of learning: doing and getting feedback. (People aren't simple; all four stages overlap!).

Learning by doing
- the heart of open learning

Surprising as it is to many people in the world of education (and not surprising at all to trainers), people don't learn much by sitting at the feet of the master or mistress. In addition, people don't learn much just by *reading* the fine words of experts. People learn by having a go themselves. They learn by *doing*. They learn by getting things right. They learn even more by getting things wrong - and getting feedback on what was wrong. It's particularly helpful to learn by getting things wrong *in the comfort of privacy* - one of the most powerful strengths of open learning.

'Doing' is more than just 'recalling'

Designing an open learning package is essentially a case of designing things for learners to do, from which they can learn. Admittedly, sometimes we have to tell them a little information before they can do something useful - though usually this information can be quite minimal. Sadly, writers too often feel that they have to write down everything that they know - not much help to people who learn by doing, not reading.

What can learners do?

It's not just a matter of giving learners some information, then giving them the chance to tell it back to you. Here are a few ideas, all of which can be built into tasks for learners to do: deciding, choosing, prioritising, summarising, arguing, defending, attacking, backing, proposing, creating, suggesting, illustrating, explaining, expressing, discussing, planning, exploring, fault-finding, criticising, evaluating.

How soon should the 'doing' begin?

As soon as possible! It's often possible to begin an open learning package with something interesting for learners to do - for example to map out what they can already do (and can't yet do) using a checklist. When learning-by-doing is built into a package right from the start, learners quickly get the idea that the package is not just another text book.

Self-assessment questions, activities, assignments

As soon as learners have a go at some 'learning by doing' they need to be able to find out 'was I right?' or 'was my choice a sensible one?'. So, any good learning activity will be one where it is possible to learn by doing *and* it will also be possible to learn by getting feedback on what has been done. In short, the most important parts of any open learning package are those learners *that do,* not just read.

Getting the tasks right

When you're there in person to tell people what to do, they've got more than your words to help them work out *exactly* what they should be trying to do. They've got your tone of voice. There's your facial expression. There's your body language. When you're writing tasks for open learners to do, the words need to be particularly well-chosen, to compensate for all those other clues that aren't available to learners. The best way to get the wording of tasks right is to try the written tasks out on 'live' people in a face-to-face situation, watching how they respond to the words and asking them whether the purposes of the tasks are clear.

Learning from feedback

Throughout this book I've mentioned this. Learners need feedback to help them feel good about what they have just learned successfully - and to help them find out what they have not yet learned successfully. When learners have a go at self-assessment questions or activities, they need a lot more than mere *answers.* Look at it this way: all they can tell from an answer is whether they were right or not. True, that's feedback of sorts. But it's possible to give much more useful feedback if we try to *respond to what learners do.* In other words, if we ask them to make a choice, we need to be able to comment on whether they made a good choice *and* explain the justification supporting the best choice *and* explain to anyone making a different choice exactly what is wrong with doing that.

Praise and sympathy

When people do something well, it helps enormously to say 'well done'. There are thousands of ways of wording 'well done' messages - there's no need to be repetitious and boring about giving praise.

When people get something wrong, especially working alone as open learners, they need a few well chosen words of 'sympathy' along with the explanations to help them on their way. The danger is that someone who gets something wrong may be thinking *'am I the only idiot in the world who would have got this wrong?'* Words such as *'this was a tricky question'* or *'most people have trouble with this at first'* can make all the difference.

Write 'responsable' questions

Sorry about the shock of a 'new' word that looks very much like a spelling mistake, but I've found it a useful term to use in open-learning writing workshops - people remember it! By 'responsable', I simply mean 'able to be responded to'. The need for feedback places limits on the sorts of questions which can be useful to learners. It's little use asking them to *list four causes of inflation*. They may list four completely different ones from the ones we want them to list - and they may be right. Far better to ask them *which of the following are the four most important causes of inflation?* (giving eight possibilities, say), then responding exactly why four are more important than the others, and including explanations of any of the possibilities they may have chosen which are not causes of inflation at all.

Various sorts of feedback

Learners can benefit from printed feedback comments which *respond* to what they do with self-assessment questions or activities. They can also benefit from 'human' feedback, for example that given by a tutor responding to a tutor-marked assignment. However, there are even more possibilities for ensuring that learners get sufficient feedback to make them feel good about their learning.

Other people can be a vital resource. Learners can give feedback to each other. Friends, supervisors, bosses, managers, employees, and all sorts of other people can be a resource to learners regarding getting feedback. Learners may indeed need help in working out who to ask what, for feedback.

Help learners to receive feedback well

'There is no such thing as criticism, there is just feedback' - if only it were as easy as this. However, it can make all the difference if some time can be spent with learners convincing them of the value of feedback even when it is 'negative'. Simply helping them to receive critical comment as 'criticism of something I did' rather than 'criticism of me' is a major step.

Digesting - making the learning one's own

Some revered theorists of learning have referred to this as 'reflection'. For years, I happily went along with them. To learn something, we do indeed need to make sense of it, take stock of it, and allow it to fit in among all the other things we know. However, the more I thought about it, the less-happy I became with the word 'reflection' for these processes. 'Reflection' implies something rather passive. And in any case, a mirror only gives one back what is placed before it (the wrong way round horizontally, yet alright vertically - no wonder 'reflection' can cause confusion!).

Then I thought of *digesting*. This useful word describes what we really want to help people do to consolidate their learning. It implies 'making it one's own'. It implies taking stock and making sense of what has been learned. It implies giving it time. It implies sorting it out into what one needs to keep - and discarding in due course the parts that are not useful or relevant. Sadly, our education system does not seem to have been good at helping digestion. In particular, we tend to have tried to 'fill people up' with all sorts of things they don't really need and not faced up to the need for them to sort out what they needed, then dispose of the rest. Perhaps (to take the analogy one step too far?) there are a lot of people who steer clear of opportunities to learn simply because they have become constipated?

Summaries and reviews

These can be a big help in the 'digesting' stage. Summaries and reviews help learners to decide what they need to retain. It can even be useful to read the summary or review *before* starting a topic as a way of finding out what it's *really* going to be about (especially if the objectives aren't clearly spelled out). Sadly, many open learning materials are skimpy on summaries or reviews. However, it's relatively easy - and very useful - to 'add-on' summaries and reviews by writing study-guide material to help learners to navigate an existing open learning resource.

'Hiccups'

If we overload our digestive systems, hiccups give us a useful message. The same can be true of learning. It is possible to build into open learning materials, from time to time, an activity that will 'catch' anyone who is going at it too fast and help them to consolidate things they really need.

Indigestion remedies

Every now and then, a good open learning package will give learners the chance to find out how their 'digesting' is going. This can take the form of an exercise which helps them to detect any parts that are not being properly digested, offering helpful suggestions about how to go about putting the situation right.

Supporting open learners

In this short chapter, I've been concentrating on those components of learning packages which can help open learners to learn productively, using their natural ways of learning. However, even the best open learning package can work even better if it is well supported from 'outside' - for example by tutors or mentors. Human helpers can be even more responsive than print when it comes to providing learners with feedback on what they have done. Moreover, human helpers can help maintain open learners' motivation - in other words, 'keep them *wanting* to learn'.

Summary

When designing open learning materials - whether print-based, computer-based, or multimedia packages - what matters is 'how it works'. This is much more important than the 'content' of the materials. The keys to quality are the elements of the materials which mesh with the ways that people actually learn. The best materials will create the *want* to learn, provide abundant opportunities to *learn by doing,* provide a great deal of useful *feedback* to learners and take account of the fact that learning does not happen instantly, but needs time for *digestion*.

Chapter 9

Towards flexible learning quality
- Moving from traditional teaching to flexible learning

Abstract

This chapter aims to help teachers develop flexible learning materials from the resources they already use with their students. The chapter suggests how to make an 'additionality' approach at least as effective as employing off-the-shelf flexible learning resource materials. This chapter contains various ideas relating to moving teaching-learning processes towards open, flexible or distance learning.

When you've applied these ideas to your own situation, I hope you'll be better-able to:

- decide whether to adopt, adapt, or start from scratch, as you track down and examine existing flexible learning materials in your subject areas.

- work out *which* of the materials you are already using in your teaching lend themselves to being adapted into something that will work as a flexible learning resource.

- build on existing resources at your disposal, adding to them components which will allow them to work in independent-study mode.

- choose or develop high quality flexible learning resources.

Flexible, open and distance learning

Each of these terms has been defined in different ways by different writers. Perhaps the simplest way to explain the similarities, differences, and overlaps between them is to describe how the respective types of learning usually happen.

Towards flexible learning quality

Distance learning

Learners are separated by distance from providers for some, most, or even all of the time. Examples include the Open University (UK), various correspondence learning agencies, and some in-company training schemes where trainees are studying at their own base rather than in a training centre. Usually (but not always) distance learning is done by people working on their own.

Open learning

This term is broader, and includes all the examples of distance learning given above. Open learning usually means that learners have some control over three primary factors: time, place and pace, or in other words

- where they learn
- when they learn
- how they learn

'Open learning' can sometimes also be taken to mean 'open to all comers'. For example, the Open University takes people without the formal entry qualifications required by many traditional institutions of higher education. However, in practice, most open learning programmes need learners to have already reached particular levels of competence or experience, as laid down in the 'prerequisite knowledge and skills' listed in the materials.

Flexible learning

This term is even broader, and includes all forms of open and distance learning, but also includes other learning situations which at first sight appear more traditional. For example, 200 people in a lecture theatre can be 'learning flexibly', if (for example) they are spending five minutes where everyone is working through a handout and trying to answer some questions. In other words, flexible learning involves people taking some control regarding how they learn. Flexible Learning should be considered as part of a toolkit of ways of developing successful learning outcomes and demonstrable competences in our students. Essentially, developing flexible learning processes from traditional teaching processes is largely a matter of putting into print not only the content of the syllabus, but particularly the *support* which would be offered to the students by teachers. Since it is recognised that most learning occurs by *doing*, the key aspect of the development of flexible learning resource materials is the *interaction* between learners and materials - in particular how well the materials respond to learners' attempts to answer self-assessment questions.

'Doing' and 'feedback' in flexible learning

Important aspects of the support and interaction which can be built in to flexible learning resources are:

- the *tasks and exercises* whereby learners gain competence
- the *feedback* learners receive on their progress
- the *guidance* learners are given regarding use of textbooks and resources
- details of the *assessment criteria* which will be indicative of successful outcomes.

Towards flexible learning quality

The end of traditional teaching?

It is not suggested that flexible learning should replace all traditional teaching. For many purposes, face-to-face learning situations have advantages over learning alone, and peer group interaction is a vital part of many kinds of learning. In particular, it is possible to arrange that learners receive feedback from their peers - far more feedback than could be received from tutors or lecturers (even if not the 'expert' feedback which they need in addition). It would be sensible to examine which parts of our curriculum are best handled through each of several alternatives including:

- large-group teaching and learning
- small-group tutorial work
- small-group unsupervised work
- individual self-study on campus
- individual self-study at a distance
- small-group self-study.

Each of these learning situations should be used for those purposes particularly suited to it. For those curriculum elements where self-study pathways or components are feasible and desirable, we can develop or acquire flexible learning resources of a suitable quality and standard.

By far the best situation in which to develop flexible learning resource materials is by being involved face-to-face with 'traditional students'. The ultimate aim may be to produce resources which can promote learning without the presence of a tutor, but the handover of control is best done one step at a time, with thorough monitoring of each move towards learner autonomy.

A longer-term aim should be to establish distance learning pathways, built initially from those flexible learning resources which prove their worth with conventional students.

Ten reasons for moving towards flexible learning

1   Increasing competition between institutions of higher education and training means that we have to be able to *cater more flexibly* for a wide variety of student needs and expectations.

2   With increased need for *collaboration* between providers of education and training, resource-based learning provides an easier basis for such collaboration.

3   The availability of a substantial proportion of curricula in *packaged* form significantly helps progress towards a modular structure and allows increased choice to students.

4   Increased pressure on funding will mean we need to be able to cater both for *larger class numbers* and for *new target groups* of part-time and distant students.

5   As the proportion of *mature and non-traditional entry students* increases, we need to complement traditional teaching and learning approaches by creating additional flexible learning pathways and to replace entirely some traditional approaches disliked by mature students.

6   With increasing use of supported self-study in secondary education, *student expectations* are likely to move away from that of being taught mostly in lectures.

7   With the increased franchising of our programmes in further education colleges and in-company training departments, the availability of flexible learning resource materials provides an excellent means of ensuring that the *quality of learning* is maintained and controlled.

8   In *commerce and industry,* open and flexible learning is becoming much more attractive than traditional training (many central training departments have been restructured or even closed down).

9   It is increasingly realised that, in many disciplines, higher education students are *seriously 'over-taught'*, and that this produces surface rather than deep learning and limits students' development of highly valued transferable skills.

10   Perhaps the most important outcome of higher education should be the development of *the ability to manage one's own learning*; flexible learning pathways develop this ability - being taught inhibits such development.

Adopt, adapt, or start from scratch?

- *Does something suitable exist already?*
  If the 'perfect' open learning materials (perfect for your learners' needs) exist already, the most logical thing would seem to be to **Adopt** them. This may mean negotiating with whoever owns the materials to get quantity-discounts. If (as is often the case) there are materials which **Nearly** meet your learners' needs, you may well be able to 'make up' any deficiencies with tutorial support, or with things you add-on to the materials. There are various catalogues and databases which can be valuable in helping to identify and locate materials which already exist. However, there is no substitute for getting your hands on existing materials, before deciding whether they can be used as they are, or whether they lend themselves to adaptation for your students. You may need to use all the tricks you can think of to get a good look at such materials. Better still, it's worth trying a small-scale pilot before committing yourself to the purchase of large quantities of materials. Another way of tracking down potentially relevant learning materials is through informal contacts with colleagues from other institutions. Coffee-breaks at conferences can be very profitable if used to help find people with whom you can exchange resources and information! A good checklist should be useful in helping you decide which materials may be good enough to adopt. You could use the checklist at the end of this chapter as a starting point and refine it to tune-in better to the needs of your learners.

- *Have you time to start from scratch?*
  Writing open learning materials from scratch takes time - a lot of time! Open learning writing has often been paid for on the basis of ten hours to write up the equivalent of one hour's learning. In practice, it may take more like a hundred hours to write up one hour of learning, when preparation, piloting, editing, adjusting and so on are taken into account. If something fairly close to what is needed already exists, it can be more economical to adapt rather than start from scratch. However, you'll learn many valuable things from having a go at writing your own materials. If you really **want** to create new materials, the time issue seems to take care of itself.

- *Could the 'not invented here syndrome' affect you?*
  Most teachers and trainers feel a little uncomfortable working with materials written by others. We tend to prefer to work with materials where we have a sense of 'ownership'. Even if alternative materials are better than our own, our instinct is to prefer our own, and it's only too easy for us to see all sorts of weaknesses in other people's materials. This can be a reason for starting from scratch and writing new flexible learning resource materials. However, the *real* reason should be based on the needs of our learners. If these needs are best served by writing new materials specially for them, starting from scratch is indeed justified.

What are the advantages of *adapting*?
Adapting existing resource materials can have many advantages, including the following:

- it can save time and expense.
- you probably already own materials which can be adapted.
- you can adapt materials a bit at a time.
- you may be able to try out the adapted bits face-to-face with conventional classes to gain feedback and enable improvements to be made quickly.
- you *may* be able to use small pieces of published material without copyright problems or payments - but seek expert help and advice. Librarians often know a lot about copyright rules and regulations.
- you'll still feel a considerable amount of 'ownership' of the materials if you've done all the fine-tuning yourself (i.e. avoiding the 'not invented here' feeling).
- it can be much less expensive than having to purchase complete packages for each of your learners.
- adapting can be excellent practice towards writing some materials from scratch in due course.

'Learning by Doing' - the heart of flexible learning

Most learning happens when we actually try to *do* something. Learning doesn't happen efficiently when we merely read about something or listen to someone talk about it. The measure of a good open learning package is *what the students do* as they work through it. Therefore, preparing to put together an open learning package (or adapting something which exists already) is *not* so much a matter of collecting together all the things students need to read - it's about collecting together a set of things for students to *do*.

Towards flexible learning quality

When you already teach a subject face-to-face, you are likely to have a considerable collection of tasks and activities you give your students - in other words you are already well on your way to having one of the most important ingredients of your open learning packages. Don't forget the words you say when you introduce a task to students. Though you may already use printed sheets for the task briefings, any additional verbal briefing is likely to play a very important part in helping students see exactly what they are intended to do as they approach a task. With verbal briefing you have the additional advantages of tone of voice, emphasis, facial expression and body language. When translating tasks for flexible learning usage, it helps considerably if you can capture as many of these 'extra dimensions' as possible and wrap them up somehow in printed words.

What have I already, that can be used or adapted?

When you're already teaching a subject using traditional or face-to-face methods, it is not a mammoth task to translate your experience into the design of flexible learning resource materials, particularly if you are able to make the transition a little at a time. For example, it is possible to translate small elements of your normal teaching into flexible learning mode and try them out in traditional lectures or tutorials, gaining feedback from your observations of how your learners get on with the materials, questions, and feedback. Also, you can design mini-modules to give to learners, covering things you decide *not* to do in face-to-face mode.

The list below is an attempt to show how well you are 'armed' for making the transition towards flexible delivery of subjects you already teach. You will have many of the following - and probably more:

- Your experience of teaching - probably the most valuable resource in this list.
- Your knowledge of students' problems.
- Your ability to help students to find solutions to their problems.
- Syllabus objectives or competences you work with already.
- Your own handout materials;
    - usually no copyright problems.
    - often already contain central material.
- Existing resource materials.
- Class exercises
    - often adaptable to make self-assessment questions.
- Case study details
    - usually already the basis for learner activity - the essential part of flexible learning.
- Your own lecture notes
    - these may cover most of the content your learners need, already in concise form.
- Textbook extracts
    - it may be possible to obtain clearance to include small extracts without charge.
    - OR it may be possible to get learners to refer to books (bought or borrowed from libraries)

- Manuals
  - usually are already some way towards being interactive material
  - it may be possible to use extracts without copyright difficulties
  - it may be easy to re-compose extracts to avoid copyright difficulties
  - it may be possible to refer learners to 'available' manuals directly
- worksheets and assignments you give your students already
- problems and projects you design for your students

What may need *adding* for flexible-learning usage?

Some or all of the principal features of the best open learning materials can be added to transform your existing materials into flexible learning resources.

User-friendly objectives
- warming up things like 'the expected learning outcome is that the student will...' to 'by the end of .... you'll be able to.....'
- making objectives more directly relevant to learners' needs
- making them appropriate to the assessment criteria involved

RESPONSES to questions/tasks/activities
- not just model answers, but RESPONSES to what learners DO when they have a go at the questions/tasks/activities.
- discussion of anticipated errors/difficulties
- positive, encouraging comments for learners who have succeeded
- reassuring and encouraging comments for learners who did not succeed

ADDITIONAL questions/tasks/activities
- in self-assessment format, with responses as above

Written study-skills help
- the sorts of help and support you'd give face-to-face learners informally.

Assessment criteria
- to link with objectives, learning outcomes and performance standards.
- to alert learners to what counts and what could lose them credit.
- to build learners' confidence, allowing them insight into 'the rules of the game'

Summaries/reviews/checklists
- provide 'repeats' of crucial points, allowing learners to see what is most important.
- provide useful revision aids.

Feedback questionnaires
- these should be short, structured, and in easy-to-complete format, but with additional space for comments from learners who *want* to expand on the basic questions.

Audiotape commentaries and discussions
- relatively cheap and simple to produce.
- can make it less lonely for learners working on their own.
- can be useful for talking learners through things like textbook extracts, derivations, complex diagrams and so on.
- can also be used to help learners self-assess more complex tasks they may have done as part of their work - i.e. talking them through good answers and common mistakes (can be more friendly than a long printed response).

BRIEFINGS showing learners how best to use external resources such as textbooks, manuals, audiotapes, video, or practical kits.

How can a package be put together efficiently?

Turning your existing resources into an open learning package can be done more easily than you might have imagined. It's best to get the various separate components of your package into good working order, trying them out with groups of your students whenever you can, then gradually build the components together into a draft package and see how your students cope with it.

At first, the task of putting together an open learning package may seem formidable - especially if you want to equal the best published packages. However, Rome wasn't built in a day, and the best open learning materials were created gradually, step by step - with a great deal of piloting at each stage.

Most of these steps are simple extensions of things you do in your day-to-day work with your students.

The following sequence can save much time and trouble.

1   Design *self-assessment questions* and *activities* for your open learners, based on the class-work exercises you presently use and the assignments and projects you set your existing students, linking these to the syllabus *objectives* or *competences* in the same way as you already do.

      Adjust the wording of all these components as you go, so they become as straightforward and clear as possible, so that learners don't need you to explain what the words mean.

2   Write *responses* to each self-assessment question and activity. Base these responses on the way you deal with your live students. Write in the explanations you give them when they make mistakes.

      Keep striving to make the questions and responses as self-explanatory as you can so that you don't need to be present in person. Try out each draft with your live students and observe any difficulties, adjusting questions and responses as necessary.

3   Start turning your notes and handouts into short sections of text. Make these sections bridge the gaps between the *response* to one question and the next question. Each chunk of text therefore has a distinct function - to lead up to the next student activity.

4   When there are questions or activities which really do need a human response rather than a pre-prepared one, turn the questions into *tutor marked assignments* and build these in to your package.

5   Go through the bits and pieces of your package, adding **summaries** or **reviews** at key points. Make such additions every time your students may need reinforcement of principal ideas and concepts.

6   Now that your package is nearing a 'working' form, go through it again, adding **short introductions** or **'lead-in'** paragraphs, preparing your students for what is to come in each part. It's far easier to write well-tuned introductions when you've already written the parts you're leading up to.

As you can see from the above sequence, writing an open learning package is not done in the same way as writing a textbook. It's not a matter of starting by writing page 1 and working through in a linear sequence.

Open learning packages are designed around the **learning** that students will gain from them. This takes the emphasis away from the text itself and means you don't need to try to write everything you know about the subject, only the things your students **need** to gain.

It's often advisable to start working on the middle of your package, then work outwards in both directions. Writing the very beginning is one of the most crucial tasks - this is much easier to do if you've already written later parts of the package - you know then exactly what you're introducing.

Responses - not just answers

The responses you write for self-assessment questions and activities are by far the most important ingredient of your open learning package and therefore you should give them careful attention. (It's sadly all-to-easy to tell that questions and responses have been added to many open learning packages at the last minute - almost as an afterthought).

If you think about the best quality face-to-face teaching, some of the most important skills include:

- explaining to students what to do when they can't yet answer a question
- helping students to feel a glow when they do something correctly
- helping students find out exactly what went wrong when they make mistakes.

Writing open learning materials gives you the chance to package up these valuable skills, so that your help is extended to students even when you're not there in person. The response to a good self-assessment question should enable each student to find out two things:

'was I right?'
'if not, why not?'

When open learning materials are scrutinised by professional open learning writers, the first thing that they turn to are the responses to self-assessment questions and activities. If these responses are working well, the package is a good one.

Structured questions are easier to respond to!

Responding to open-ended questions is possible - but usually difficult. A good response needs to cover every answer that learners may reasonably have given - and more. Structured questions involve learners making a decision such as:

- which is the correct option?
- which is the most sensible course of action?
- which is the best order in a sequence?

With such questions, you can respond directly to learners who choose a 'wrong' or 'less-good' option, explaining exactly why their choice is not the best one.

Some guidelines for briefings

'Briefings' represent one area of support and advice that is normally handled quite informally in face-to-face sessions. Students at such sessions have the extra advantages of tone-of-voice and facial expression, helping them find out more about exactly what they're intended to do with the textbooks and literature references they're given. The same level of support needs to be put into print if students studying by flexible learning pathways are to derive the same amount of benefit from briefings to resource materials. The following suggestions give some ways of ensuring that printed briefings serve learners effectively.

- *Keep them short and specific:* it is better to have briefings to *short extracts* than to whole books or chapters:
  e.g. 'Now work through Sections 2.3 and 2.5' is better than 'Now read Chapter 2'.

- *Make briefings ACTIVE,* i.e. don't just ask learners to 'read' things, but give them things to do WHILE they read them - or even BEFORE reading things (not just after they've read them).

- *Include 'Commentary' elements in briefings*
  e.g. 'Chapter 3 gives a good overview of ...., watch out particularly for the way .... is discussed. Don't worry about .... at this stage, you don't need to know the sort of detail that you'll see in Section 3.5!'

- *Include 'signposting' in briefings*
  e.g. 'In Section 4.8 we've already seen why .... happens. In Section 4.9 you'll find out what happens when ...., which is useful when you need to work out how to ....'

- *Plant QUESTIONS in learners' minds*
  When learners have already got some questions in mind before reading something, they have a subconscious 'thirst' for the answers to the questions. This means that when they come across the 'answers' as they read, those parts are more memorable to them. This makes reading far more efficient.

Towards flexible learning quality

e.g. 'As you study Section 6, try to find answers to the following three questions:

Why does ....?
How could ....?
When might you find ....?

- ### Include 'STEERING' in briefings
  e.g. 'You don't need to spend much time on Section 7 unless you WANT to'
  'The heart of the matter is explained very well near the end of Section 5.7'
  'Aim to spend about half an hour simply getting the feel of Chapter 4 before having a go at the next set of self-assessment questions'.

- ### Help learners to find out for themselves which parts they need to concentrate on
  This can be done by using self-assessment questions to measure how much different learners already know about a topic and by using the Responses to route each learner accordingly.

For example:
Before you move on to Chapter 3 of the textbook, have a go at SAQ 23 below.

SAQ 23
Before studying 'waldefaction' in Jones and Smith, have a go at the following six questions to see if you already know something about it (don't worry if not - it's all in Jones and Smith!)

-
-
-
-
-
-

Response to SAQ 23 *(out of sight of the question)*
- *(correct answers)*
-
-
-
-
-

If you got all of these right - well done - and you only need to look at Sections 3.7 and 3.9 in Chapter 3; you already know all you need to from the other sections.

If your only mistake was to ...., you'll find out what to do about it at the beginning of Section 3.2. The only other parts of Chapter 3 you should give particular attention to are Sections 3.7 and 3.9.....

If you didn't get much of this SAQ right - don't worry - it's all covered in Chapter 3. As you work through this Chapter, take particular note of Sections 3.2 and 3.4 - these contain what you need to do questions like SAQ 23...........

Writing study guides

Some flexible learning programmes hardly 'contain' any subject matter in the normal sense of the term, but are written to guide learners through an existing resource such as a 'reader', or through a selection of resource materials. The Open University, for example, often adopts key reference books as the major source of information in a course. The open learning packages then become interactive guides to the books. All that I said earlier about briefings continues to apply to this sort of guidance. It remains particularly important that when learners have completed a task or activity based on the reference material, the study guide provides them with true responses to what they have been doing.

The 'books plus study guide' format solves several problems. Copyright is taken care of, as learners purchase (or are loaned) the original source material. Economies of scale are possible, as mass-produced books tend to be less expensive than open learning modules produced in runs of only hundreds. Any study guide is much slimmer than the corresponding material would have been if it had been put together in fully-interactive open learning style.

The study guide format depends, of course, on the availability of the resources to be used. If a text-book goes out of print, or becomes dated and superseded by new work, the study-guide will at once be redundant. However, it remains less expensive to revise or renew a 'slim' study guide than to redesign a full open learning module.

Some general tips for writers

- Avoid sitting thinking about writing - write! Set yourself stage deadlines - better still, let other people know about your deadlines. Work on small manageable jobs - don't try to work on the whole package at once.

- Show your writing to other people (students, colleagues, friends) long before it's 'ready'. Critical feedback on an early draft is easier to swallow than criticism of your completed masterpiece.

- Keep the tone relatively informal. Use *'you'* for your students. Use *'I'* as the author. As far as you can, try to make the printed page 'talk' to your students in the same way as you would have talked yourself - particularly when explaining things.

- Remind yourself now and then that you're not writing a major treatise, or a paper for an esteemed journal in your field. You're writing for your students. Don't stand on your professional dignity in your writing.

- Use plenty of *white space*. Leave room for your students to write into the material their answers to your questions and their own notes and comments. Your students will develop an important sense of ownership of the materials as they write all over them.

- Use short words rather than long words where possible. Get your meaning across as directly as you can (there's no 'tone-of-voice' or 'facial expression' to help your open learners).

- Use short simple sentences rather than long complex ones. Aim to get your meaning across on the first reading of each sentence. Be particularly careful when setting questions and tasks. Make sure that students will know exactly what they are intended to do with each task.

- Include headings and sub-headings so that students can see at a glance what each page is doing. If your students can see where they're going - and where they've been - their journey through your open learning package will be more likely to be successful.

- Include illustrations wherever they help students to understand things. Illustrations also help to keep students going - a page with something visual on it looks more enticing than a solid page of text.

Piloting - the best guarantee of quality

You may have seen many open learning materials which *look* marvellous - but which don't work! These are packages which were 'glossed-up' and published long before they were ready.

The more feedback you can get about how your package works, the better you can make your final version. The best open learning packages owe as much to the experiences of students who tested them out, as to the skills of the authors.

You don't have to wait until you've got a finished-product before starting to gather feedback. You can try out each small part as you compose it. For example, with the help of your students, you can test your self-assessment questions and responses. You can try out your tutor-marked assignments. You can change things every time you find a problem.

When eventually you have a first draft of your package assembled, it's useful to try this out on some students (and on some. colleagues), deliberately seeking detailed feedback by providing questionnaires (and by talking to your piloteers).

Among other things, make sure you ask questions such as:

'What is the best thing about the package?'

'What do you like least about the package?'

'What do you think is the hardest part of the package?'

'What do you think of the tone and style of the package?'

'How clear are the objectives of the package?'

'How useful are the self assessment questions and activities?'

'How helpful are the responses to the self assessment questions and activities?'

'Do you think there are sufficient illustrations?'

'How useful are the summaries and reviews?'

'How long do you think the package takes to work through?'

'Suggest some changes which can improve the package'.

A checklist for flexible learning resources

The checklist which follows is quite powerful! If all the answers are 'yes' or 'very well indeed', you're looking at an exemplary piece of open learning material. However, even when some of the criteria below are not met, all is not lost. In fact, it's very useful to identify exactly which criteria aren't met by a particular piece of flexible learning material; you are then in a position to compensate for whatever's lacking. It often only takes a few extra words or lines to 'plug a gap' in some material, or to help learners to make better use of it.

If you are writing your own material, you should find this checklist a useful self-editing resource. I've clustered the 30 checklist questions under sub-headings representing the main elements of flexible learning materials identified earlier in this chapter.

Objectives or statements of intended learning outcomes
1 Is there a clear indication of any prerequisite knowledge or skills?
2 Are the objectives stated clearly and unambiguously?
3 Are the objectives presented in a friendly way? (i.e. *not* 'the expected learning outcomes of this module are that the student will...........'!)
4 Do the objectives avoid 'jargon' which may not be known to learners before starting the material?

Structure and layout
5 Is the material visually attractive?
6 Is there sufficient white space? (for learners to write notes, answer questions, do calculations, and so on).
7 Is it easy for learners to find their way backwards and forwards? This is sometimes called 'signposting' and includes good use of headings.

Self-assessment questions and activities
8 Are there plenty of them? (Remember that flexible learning - like any other learning in fact - is largely dependent on 'learning by doing').
9 Are the tasks set by the questions clear and unconfusing?

10   Are the questions and tasks inviting? (Is it clear to learners that it's valuable for them to have a go rather than skip?)

11   Is there enough space for learners to write their answers?

12   Collectively, do the self assessment questions and activities test learners' achievement of the objectives?

Responses to self-assessment questions and activities

13   Are they really *responses to what the learner has done?* (i.e. not just answers to the questions).

14   Do the responses meet the learners' need to find out:
'Was I right?'
'If not, why not?'

15   Do the responses include encouragement or praise (without patronising) for learners who got them right?

16   Do the responses include something that will help learners who got it wrong *not* to feel like complete idiots?

Introductions, summaries and reviews

17   Is each part introduced in an interesting, stimulating way?

18   Do the introductions alert learners to the way the materials are designed to work?

19   Is there a clear and useful summary/review?

20   Does it provide a useful way to revise the material quickly?

The text itself

21   Is it readable and unambiguous?

22   Is it relevant? (for example, does it keep to the Objectives as stated?)

23   Is it 'involving' where possible? (i.e. plenty of use of 'you' for the learner, 'I' for the author, 'we' for the learner and author together)

Diagrams, charts, tables, graphs, and so on

24   Is each as self-explanatory as possible?

25   Does the learner know what to do with each? (i.e. *to learn it, to note it in passing, to pick out the trend, or even nothing at all)*

26   'A sketch can be more useful than 1000 words': is the material sufficiently illustrated?

Some general points

27   Is the material broken into manageable chunks?

28   Does the material avoid any sudden jumps in level?

29   Does the material ensure that the average learner will achieve the objectives?

30   Will the average learner *enjoy* using the material?

Helping learners use flexible learning materials

The following suggestions can help learners adjust their approach to using flexible or open learning materials. I suggest that you fine-tune and develop your own advice to your learners, starting from the list below, by adding-in comments relating to the particular style and format of the materials they will be using.

Towards flexible learning quality

1   Check whether there are things you should already be able to do before you start working through the open learning materials. Information such as 'prerequisites' is often given at the start.

2   If the material gives **objectives** one way or another, pay particular attention to these and keep returning to see how well you are getting on towards mastering them. Objectives are usually phrased along the lines 'when you've completed this package, you should be able to.........'

3   Most open learning materials (good ones) are 'active' and contain things for you to do as you work through them. These active parts are sometimes called **self-assessment questions** or **activities.** However tempted you are to skip these and read on, don't skip them! Even if you think you know the answer, jot it down, **then** compare what you did with the answer or response given in the material.

4   When you get a question right, be pleased with yourself. When you get one wrong, be even more pleased - you've found out something useful. Find out exactly **why** you didn't get the right answer - and remember this for next time.

5   When you come to a bit that has you stumped, don't struggle with it for ages. Skim ahead and see what's coming next. The next bit may be straightforward. Make a note of exactly what you don't understand about the bit that stumped you, and plan to find out from someone how to deal with that bit. It's probably quite simple when you've got someone who can explain it to you, even though you may never have worked it out on your own.

6   Open learning materials often contain a great deal of information - don't try to learn it all as you proceed. Make decisions about what is required to be learned, as opposed to the things you are merely required to understand as you read them. It's very useful to work with fellow students for this - you'll all have slightly different views about exactly what is important and what isn't - the truth will be closer to the average than to one person's view.

7   If you've been given your own copy of the open learning material, make it **belong** to you, by writing your own comments and notes all over it (as well as by writing in the answers to questions and activities). You'll often remember the things you added to the material - a useful way of boosting what you remember about the topics involved.

8   Keep looking back - remind yourself of the things you've already done. The more often these things have been through your mind the more firmly you'll understand them.

9   Keep glancing ahead to see what's coming next. You'll often understand **why** you're doing something only when you see where it's leading towards.

10   Have another go at all the self assessment questions and activities - again and again where they are difficult. Your ability to do something difficult depends more on how often you've tried doing it than on how thoroughly you did it once.

Conclusions

If you're already working face-to-face with students, you have several advantages when it comes to gradually turning parts of what you do into flexible learning resources.

- you *know* your students - i.e. one of your target audiences.
- you can *try things out* and get quick feedback on whether they work or not.
- you can turn *existing class-exercises and homework questions* into self-assessment questions and activities.
- you can turn the *feedback* you would give orally or in comments on marked work into printed responses to self-assessment questions and activities.
- you can transform *your own notes* into the textual parts of flexible learning materials.
- you can continue to use *face-to-face* sessions for the things that are difficult to wrap up in print.

Increased use of flexible learning within conventional programmes of study allows learners more opportunity to learn in 'high-quality' ways:

- learning by doing, rather than by being taught
- learning at their own pace, rather than at yours.
- learning in their own style, rather than in the way you happen to teach.
- learning again and again from their materials where necessary, rather than once as you teach.

Chapter 10

Need more mean worse?

Abstract

This somewhat provocative little article first appeared in 'The New Academic' in November 1992. In it, I look at ten ways that larger-class sizes could damage the experience of higher education, but also at ten ways that the challenges of greater numbers of students could be approached so as to improve their experience of higher education. You may notice that this chapter also links with the 'wanting, doing, feedback and digesting' model of learning that I have been promoting in several chapters of this book.

More what? Worse what?

There is little doubt that the next decade will, one way or another, see a substantial rise in the participation rates in higher education. Whether this is seen as a way of massaging the unemployment statistics, or a way of bringing the United Kingdom towards the levels already attained by major trading competitors, is somewhat academic. There will be more students. There will be more teachers - but not as many as we may feel we need to maintain standards.

What may become worse? The following possibilities spring easily to mind:
- the educational standards of higher education in the United Kingdom
- the quality of students' learning experience in higher education
- the quality of the rest of students' experiences of higher education
- the job-fulfilment of teachers in higher education

In this article I would like to start from a pessimistic viewpoint, looking at ways that 'more means worse', then turn to an opportunistic viewpoint, exploring ways that the challenge of more students can be turned to the advantage of all who participate in higher education in the United Kingdom.

Ten ways that more means worse?

1   More syllabus content

There is the danger that as we try to accommodate more and more students into higher education, we expand the content of the syllabus in every discipline, increasing the number of specialisms and trying to provide an ever-increasing range of different learning opportunities for the growing number of students. In my opinion, we are already too good at producing specialists and not good enough at equipping our students with the skills (transferable skills, enterprise skills, life skills) that they need to put the fruits of their education into practice in the real world outside our Universities.

2   More watching and listening

Students in higher education presently spend a considerable amount of their time and energy watching us and listening to us - especially in lectures. Sadly, perhaps, not much real learning is associated with such watching and listening. However, a temptation will be to accommodate the larger numbers by having ever more watching and listening - it's almost as easy to lecture to 400 as to 100.

3   More 'filled time'

The way higher education works has traditionally been dominated by timetables. These are usually 'teaching timetables', and there will probably be a move towards intensifying them. There is a tendency to measure the effectiveness of staff in higher education in terms of their teaching timetables - which may bear little relationship with the quality of the learning which results during these timetables. In fact, most students will tell you that 'the real learning' happens outside the teaching timetable. The real learning often happens as students prepare for assessment, weeks or months after 'being taught'.

4   More queueing

As it is already, students spend a great deal of time queueing. Perhaps the fact that this is already so is a symptom of the British patience with the 'queue-situation'. It is considered churlish to complain about queues. Yet queueing is time that is almost completely wasted (I say 'almost' because there is a little useful peer-group interaction in most queues). With larger numbers of students, queues in libraries, in computer centres, in laboratories, outside tutors doors, in refectories - and at the Students' Union bars - will all increase. 'More means worse' seems unavoidable here.

5   More lectures used for 'transmit-receive'

From the point of view of the traditional lecturer, the lecture situation is ideal for getting through a lot of material with a large number of students at the same time. The fact that it is usually the lecturer (and not the students) who is getting through a lot of material is often ignored (ask your students how much they retain from the average lecture). Larger numbers may mean a tendency to use lectures to do things that previously were done in more interactive ways.

6 More competition between students

There is already too much competition between students in higher education. Our best-educated people are usually very successful at competing with each other - and very unsuccessful at collaborating with each other. Can you see the effects of this in your own institution? If we accommodate more students into higher education, and retain the traditional ways of sorting them out into firsts, seconds, thirds, and also-rans, the competition will increase.

7 More boredom

When we ask students for feedback about the quality of their learning experiences, the word 'boring' sends shivers down our spines. 'How can something as fascinating as electrochemical thermodynamics be *boring?*' we ask in disbelief. We tend to avoid asking students questions where the answer 'boring' could be forthcoming. When we remind ourselves that we are dealing with highly-intelligent young people, it should come as no surprise that they find a lot of things boring. They tend to be bored most easily when they can't do anything much (except write notes) - for example in lectures and seminars. More of these will promote even more boredom.

8 More students for the same resources

In higher education today, there are seldom as many books as libraries would wish to provide. There is seldom a surplus of reading-desks where students can study. There is never a surplus of student accommodation. Computers and laboratory facilities are normally stretched. More students? You don't need me to go on.

9 More assessment (of the traditional kind)

Exams may cause students to get down and do some work, but otherwise exams are lost learning opportunities. Students hardly ever get the opportunity to get their scripts back, and to learn from their mistakes and their triumphs. Even tutor-marked assessment (such as essays, laboratory reports, projects) tends to give students far less feedback than would be desirable. If the pile of essays becomes twice as high, it is reasonable to suppose that the quality of feedback to students will diminish further.

10 More regurgitation

'Monkey see, monkey do' still applies in higher education. In many subjects (not yours, of course) it's possible for students to get by quite well by simply identifying the most important points of the subject, getting a reasonably firm (short-term) grip on them, giving them back coherently when required, then forgetting them.

Ten ways that more can mean better?

1 More emphasis on learning by doing

Not much learning happens any other way in fact. Lectures may be good at providing students with stimulation and helping develop their attitudes, but the real learning happens when students start trying to do something with the subject material. Most of students' learning-by-doing does not happen in the presence of their lecturers. Much of the learning-by-doing can happen on their own - or, even better, in small groups of students. If we place more emphasis on the value of learning-by-doing and can help students structure their learning by doing and then let them get on with it, we can accommodate more students in higher education.

Need more mean worse?

2   More opportunity to receive feedback

Students learn from the feedback they receive. They learn from the formal feedback we give them. They learn from the less-formal feedback they draw from their peer-group. With more students in higher education, they're going to have less opportunity to get that formal feedback from us. However, we can help them to become better at giving feedback to each other, and at receiving feedback from each other. We can help them to structure their need for 'expert-witness feedback' better, so that we can give them this sort of feedback more readily (instead of the rather mundane feedback we often give them).

3   More learning through collaboration

If there are more students in higher education, there is automatically more opportunity for students to collaborate with their peers. Where can we help? We can pay particular attention to designing tasks and activities which are *best done* collaboratively instead of competitively. We can help students form and maintain study syndicates. We can help them get over the hangups about needing to compete, by helping them to find out how much more they can learn collaboratively.

4   More opportunity for 'digesting'

Students need time to make sense of their learning experiences. They also need time to make sense of the feedback they receive - both from us and from each other. The time students need for this process of 'digesting' does not have staffing or resource implications. If we can free some of the time that students spend in unproductive learning situations, we can even help them increase their learning effectiveness by taking a less-active role ourselves.

5   More learning through assessing

While traditional forms of assessment may often be 'lost learning opportunities', it is possible to create forms of assessment which enhance learning. Self-assessment and peer-assessment, when developed appropriately, can allow students to think more deeply about essays they write, presentations they give, reports they write, and various other important learning outcomes. Involving students in the processes of assessment can give them a deeper insight not only into the subject matter they learn, but also into the 'rules of the game' of assessment. This can mean that even in traditional forms of assessment, students can prepare themselves better to show themselves at their best.

6   More opportunity to give feedback

Having more students in higher education increases the opportunity for us to gather feedback from them about their learning experiences. It can be as quick to give a questionnaire to 400 students as to 100 students and if we then involve students themselves in analysing and prioritising the findings from the questionnaires, it can even be quicker than doing so ourselves. The findings can then become the basis for negotiations, whereby students gain a sense of ownership of the decisions to improve their learning experiences.

7   More chance to mix and match

Modularisation and credit accumulation and transfer schemes allow greater flexibility for students. The greater the number of students, the more viable become unusual learning combinations and pathways. With careful planning, it becomes possible to offer students a great deal more ownership of their curriculum options, allowing them to capitalise on their individual strengths.

8   More value placed on existing competence

It has been said that most students spend up to half their time on things they already know. With increased numbers of students in higher education, it is clearly time to ensure that students can receive credit for things they already know, without having to participate in rituals. Students who can demonstrate that they have already mastered a topic deserve exemption from any further requirement of spending time with that topic and need to be given the opportunity to demonstrate their existing competences, as a way of enabling them to decide sensibly how best to use their time in higher education.

9   More emphasis on study skills

It is now well known that higher education does not merely measure students' intelligence or competence, but measures their ability to organise their studies effectively and efficiently. Exams tend to measure exam technique. Revision demands good time-management techniques. Written answers require good skills or expression and analysis. By providing help with the processes of studying, teachers in higher education can help students to realise their full potential. Students can be helped to be more and more self-sufficient, so that increased numbers of students can learn effectively.

10   More attention to 'wanting'

If students really *want* to learn, they are very likely to succeed. Conversely, many of the student casualties in higher education today are caused not by any lack of intellect or competence, but by a lack of motivation. Perhaps one of the most valuable roles of teachers in higher education is to create and maintain 'the want to learn', and not merely to be brokers in information. A lecture which causes most of the students present to go enthusiastically into some active learning is an example of the optimum use of the large-group teaching-learning situation.

Quality of the learning experience

In the foregoing discussion, I have limited myself to just ten ways that increased student numbers in higher education can lead to disaster or to triumph. There are many more cases to be argued in each of the two directions. If we move away from the sanctity of course content towards enhancing the processes of learning, we are likely to maximise our opportunities to use large numbers in a positive way. If we focus on learning rather than on teaching, we are on our way towards helping greater numbers of students benefit from higher education. In short, if we look after the learning, the teaching will look after itself - whatever the staff-student ratios.

(Please also see Chapter 2 of this book, which again addresses the quality of the learning experience, but this time in the context of discussions of teaching quality).

Chapter 11

Help yourself to appraisal?

Abstract

There seems to be a never-ending discussion of appraisal in higher and further education at present. This discussion is coupled with the debates about quality - quality of research, quality of teaching (and dare I say it again? quality of learning). However, much of the discussion seems to get little further than to probe the *systems* used in quality-assurance and staff development. Most institutions have gone as far as setting up systems using 'appraisal interviews'. There is probably still some way to go before there is widespread use of (or even acceptance of) systematic procedures for appraising the quality of our teaching.

Nonetheless, this chapter addresses the appraisal of teaching. However, in this chapter I'm firmly on the side of the appraisee. I hope that the contents of this chapter will help staff in higher and further education to feel better prepared to face appraisal of the quality of their teaching, by giving them an opportunity to self-appraise their own work, in the comfort of privacy.

What's new about 'appraising'?

We're skilled appraisers. An important part of our job is to appraise people - or at least some aspects of people. We appraise applicants for our courses. We design **performance indicators** for our students. We design **assessment criteria** for them. We decide what **evidence** they need to produce so that we can assess their performance. We decide what the hallmarks of **quality** may be. We decide the criteria for **excellence**. We then assess their performance - or help them to assess their own or each other's performance. We evaluate their development. But despite this familiarity with various aspects of appraisal, the prospect of our being on the receiving end is often treated with dismay.

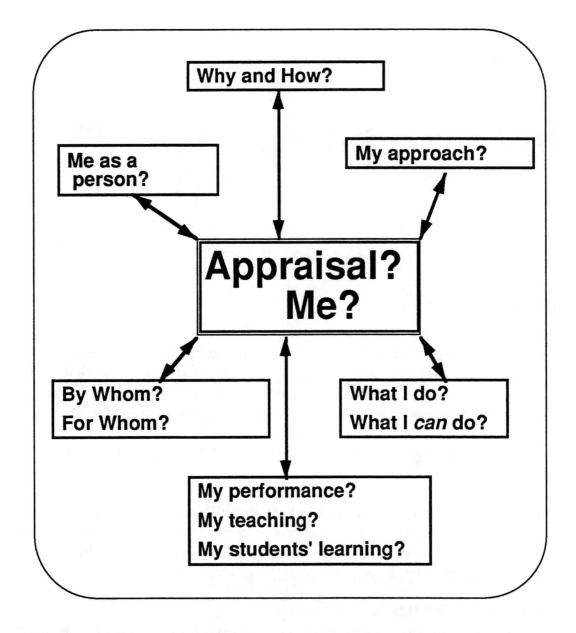

Why so emotive?

The word *appraisal* contains most of the word *praise!* Yet it would appear that the most common feeling the word appraisal engenders is to do with being found lacking. The political scene seems to be moving resolutely towards incorporating appraisal procedures into education. More importantly, there is increasing speculation that for institutions to qualify for previously-automatic funding, appraisal systems will need to be seen to be effective and the quality of teaching and learning they provide will be required to be *demonstrable* rather than 'hoped-for'. There is evidence of considerable nervousness and hostility regarding some of the possible consequences of introducing appraisal mechanisms. My purpose in this chapter is to outline some ways whereby appraisal may become more acceptable and palatable - even desirable.

We're already appraised

Throughout our careers we've been appraised! Many times. We were 'appraised' one way or another before we were appointed. We may have been appraised in one way or another if we were promoted - or if we didn't manage to be promoted. We're appraised all the time by our students - whether we like it or not. We're appraised all the time by our colleagues and managers. We may know much or little about their *findings* when they appraise us.

Appraisal does not happen only on those occasions when an additional individual carries out a structured observation of part of the work we do. Such an individual may be able to appraise some of the things we **can** do - and some of the things we **can't yet** do - but does not really have the evidence needed to appraise what we **do do** on the average day of the average week. Our colleagues and students have this evidence.

When we've been formally appraised in the past, the criteria have tended to be 'visible' or quantifiable ones, such as academic achievement, published work, research grants, administrative ability, ability to work in teams, leadership, students' success, and so on. Such criteria will continue to be part of any appraisal system.

So what's new? The new dimension is that **teaching effectiveness** is being brought more firmly into the arena. This overlaps with something more sinister perhaps - **teacher effectiveness.** In my opinion neither term is ideal - it's **learning effectiveness** measures that really count, such as the development of competences by our learners and their development of transferable skills and attributes. For many of us, performance in the classroom has tended to be something rather private - something between us and our students. Of course, that doesn't mean that teaching competence can't be appraised.

Also rather new is that appraisal is now being seen as something that should be done over a period of time. Previously, appraisal came in short, sharp instalments - on job application, applying for promotion, visits by HMI, and so on. Many of the doses of appraisal were therefore 'self inflicted'. Today's views of appraisal are more centred on a continuous and formative process - or on a regular and periodic process.

Who should do the appraising?

As I've implied, many people are already appraising us informally, including:
- students
- colleagues
- heads of department
- outsiders
- ourselves.

As more-formal systems of appraisal are set up, the appraiser could have two roles - judge and helper. There is much evidence that the second of these roles is the most important. Perhaps the role of judge is the real problem. *'What right have you lot to set yourselves up as judges of my teaching?'* is a question formulated by one of the best teachers I know. The term 'honest broker' creeps into discussions of who should appraise. An appraiser should not only help identify needs and problems, but should also provide practicable solutions to needs and problems. With the problems and undercurrents about judgments, I think the best way to start is self-appraisal; more on this later.

Who should be appraised?

Everyone! But we can't all be appraised by the same formula - we do so many different jobs. It will be important to design performance criteria relevant to all the different kinds of jobs we do. It will be necessary that selected criteria can be applied to people doing equivalent jobs in a fair and objective way. It is even more important that people being appraised have a sense of **ownership** both of the criteria against which their performance is being measured, and the processes whereby the appraisal is executed.

What should be appraised?

I've already mentioned 'performance'. This will still include activities such as research, publications, administration, teamwork and so on - but these things are relatively simple to measure. Performance will also include the more intimate processes of teaching, tutoring, assessing and preparing learning materials. After all, the things that many good teachers do best are presently seen only by their students.

Any good appraisal system is looking at **potential** as well as performance. Potential is harder to quantify, but it is very important for latent potential to be discovered and harnessed. It is probable that all of us can do things well, which we've never needed to do.

But is it really possible to measure performance and potential? Is it not the case that what we really measure is **evidence** of good performance and strong potential? Perhaps if we move the discussion away from the intangibles, people will feel less threatened by appraisal.

Defining the evidence

For example, rather than talking about measuring 'lecturing competence' let's talk about dimensions of *evidence* for competent lecturing such as:
- evidence that the lectures have been well researched and prepared.
- evidence that the material is up-to-date and relevant.
- evidence that the intended learning outcomes are clear (to the learners as well as lecturers).
- evidence that the whole of the lecture programme is planned, rather than continued week-by-week on an ad-hoc basis.
- quality of handout materials used to support a lecture programme.
- quality of overheads and other support materials.
- clarity and relevance of tasks and assignments given to learners to help them consolidate their learning.

All of the pieces of 'evidence' mentioned above can be appraised without even entering the lecture room. They can all be assembled into a teaching portfolio. However, other important elements of evidence for 'good lecturing' can only be seen at the event (or, of course, from video-recordings made of such events - these *can* be included in a teaching portfolio or profile).

- quality of presentation: audibility, clarity, manner.
- ability to maintain the attention and interest of the group.
- effective use of simple media, such as overhead projectors, blackboards, markerboards.
- effective use of more-complex media when justified, including video, computer-based resources, and so on.
- quality of the interaction between the lecturer and the group.
- nature and relevance of interaction and group work among students during lectures.
- processes of giving students the opportunity to ask questions.
- ability to respond to impromptu questions.
- processes of gathering and analysing student feedback.
- the attitude of seeking and welcoming *peer* feedback in lectures.

All people who give lectures have their own strengths and weaknesses. However, all too often, people seem somewhat afraid to ask questions which will show them what their strengths and weaknesses are - fearing, perhaps, to discover weaknesses, but at the same time denying them the opportunity of the delight of finding out unknown strengths too.

How will appraisal work?

Will it really be attempted, or will systems be built where it seems to be seen to be happening - but nothing much has changed? Will it be called *Course Monitoring* and be veiled in figures and statistics? Or will it be in the form of 'Appraisal Interviews' which may be no more than a cosy 'chat' with a Head of Department or Course Leader? Will appraisal get to the heart of the matter - the learning experiences of students? Who exactly will be pulling the appraisal strings? No-one knows yet in most institutions! This will necessarily be a topic for considerable research, discussion and negotiation.

Probably the question - and worry - in many teachers' minds is *'will someone come into my lectures, tutorials, practicals etc., and monitor what I'm doing?'* The answer may indeed be 'Yes'. However, I would hope that whenever such direct monitoring took place it would be with the purpose of helping rather than judging. I would hope it would be with the ready agreement of everyone concerned. There is plenty of experience around. Teacher training has used observation practices for decades. The new dimension may be extending such practices to teachers in normal service.

I think that people worry too much about the possibility of their privacy being invaded by someone doing some observing. This worry would be greatly reduced if observation by peers became a more everyday part of teaching. In some departments it happens without problems as a normal part of team teaching - for example when one member of staff conducts a lecture, and several others work later with small groups of students on related seminars and tutorials.

Suppose an 'average' teacher informally observes an excellent teacher at work. The average member can easily pick up ideas for improving his or her own performance. Suppose next an average teacher informally observes a poor teacher at work. Even without any criticism, the average teacher can extract from the experience some things to avoid in his or her own work. So we are bound to learn by attending others' lectures, tutorials and so on. Whether we learn things we can emulate, or things to avoid, the experience is still useful. One of the most productive ways of learning is by assessing (please see Chapter 4) - if we build in opportunities to assess each other's teaching - we're learning.

Help yourself to appraisal?

The 'threat' of observation would be considerably diminished if staff were to informally make arrangements with close or willing colleagues to sit in on each other's work from time to time.

Perhaps the real issue is **who knows?** It's alright for me to know that I gave a lousy lecture this morning. It's alright for my students to know. But it's not alright for the colleague I share a room with to know and it's definitely not alright for my Head of Department to know? And if an Appraiser finds out, *everyone* would surely get to know? However, only those who know can help! There may have been three simple matters of detail which would have made this morning's lousy lecture a quite-good lecture.

Appraising the appraisers?

If anyone should have qualms about appraisal, it is the appraisers! They will in most cases need considerable training to be able to do their job fairly and productively. It will be all to easy for appraisal processes to set up hostilities and barriers. Appraisers will also need on-going development through means for them to share their experiences. There will be the need for quality-control of appraisers! Not least, appraisers need to be receptive to feedback from their appraisees.

Do-it-yourself appraisal

I think that self-appraisal can be made to be a very important and useful part of the appraisal scene. There are dangers though. Self-Appraisal is liable to be subjective - whereas formal appraisal will at least *aim* to be objective. In Self-Appraisal, there is the danger that we confuse interest and ability. We know very well how interested we are in various aspects of our jobs. It is harder for us to tell how good we are at the different tasks we do.

I believe that a useful starting point may be a self appraisal checklist. We need the checklist to be as objective as we can make it. We need the checklist to be as relevant to our particular jobs as we can make it. In fact, to an extent, we each need to design our own checklist. However, it's easy to write a checklist including everything we know we're good at, so it will be worth including in it other ingredients - maybe from other peoples' checklists. It will be even more worthwhile for us to check out the relevance of our personal checklists with colleagues - and especially any who may find themselves doing the appraising.

The checklist approach is a means of establishing some of the performance criteria on which we may expect to be judged. Using such a checklist is an approach similar to that of students who compile a 'question-bank' of everything they may reasonably be asked in their forthcoming exams. The process is similar to encouraging students to self-assess and to assess their colleagues. The question-bank questions are short, sharp and numerous - but students who master their question banks are well-able to tackle longer exam questions - the long questions are, after all, composites of several short sharp ones. So it may be useful for us to build up a bank of short, sharp appraisal questions. We can then select from the bank those which are of particular significance to us as individuals, depending on the sort of teaching we do, the kind of subjects we teach, the sort of people who are our students - and many other factors.

Building your self-appraisal checklist

The best person to write your checklist is you! For the moment I'm simply going to supply a few 'entries' - which may or may not be directly useful to you - but which show the sort of style that a self-appraisal checklist may take. I hope you'll reply by giving me a batch of better questions. What we may end up with could be a list divided under a number of headings, such as:

- lectures
- personal tutoring
- research
- personal development

- tutorials
- teamwork
- keeping up to date

and so on.

Using self-appraisal checklists

We all have strengths and weaknesses - and will always have both. In the checklist I'm about to introduce, I'm not suggesting that the aim should be to adjust every facet of teaching overnight till our answers to every question are exemplary. I'm simply suggesting that such a checklist can be of assistance in the process of identifying the strengths and weaknesses alike. If one knows one's weaknesses at least one is in a position to tackle some of them if one wishes.

Typical questions (from various of these headings) could be something like the following. At present, only you will know how honestly you're answering any question and only you will know whether the particular question is an important one or a trivial one as far as your appraisal is concerned. I emphasise again that the following are only pointers - not an attempt at a global checklist.

Some checklist possibilities

- Do my students learn a lot during my lectures rather than later, on their own?

- Do I explain to students exactly what they are expected to become able to do?

- Do I regularly check that students have achieved stated objectives towards the end of a lecture?

- Do I use handout materials to save students merely copying what they see or hear?

- Do I maximise face-to-face contact with students to help them sort out their problems, rather than to tell them what I know?

- How often do I find myself preparing for a class in the last 24 hours before the event? Does this matter?

- Have I a bank of remedial materials ready to give to students experiencing the most common difficulties with my subject?

- Are my teaching materials designed to help students learn from them effectively?

Help yourself to appraisal?

- Do I cope well with mixed ability groups?

- What do I most like to do, and why? How important is it to my students?

- What do I least like to do, and why? Would it be better if someone else did this?

- What new teaching skills have I explored recently? Have I tried them out?

- When did I last use a book or paper on the teaching of my subject (rather than a subject book)? What was it?

- What did I learn about teaching - good or bad - from the last Conference presentation I observed?

- What new teaching skills should I explore next? Is there anyone who can help me?

- What is the longest time I've used a particular set of notes or handouts without revision?

- Are my handouts reasonably professionally laid out, or do they look like hasty copies of some notes?

- Are overhead transparencies I use often of a reasonable quality? Can all of them be seen from the back of the room?

- What differences in approach do I use for lectures, tutorials, and one-to-one encounters with students?

- What has been the most successful part of my recent teaching? Why was this?

- What has been the worst thing that happened recently in my teaching? What did I learn from this which will help me prevent this from happening again?

- Am I sufficiently good at administration, keeping records, and so on?

- How quickly on average do I return marked work? Is this quick enough?

- Do I put constructive comments on poor work, or do I just give a low grade?

- Do I remember to give some praise to students whose work is really good? Do I write 'well done' as often as I should?

- How many of my students do I know by name? Is this reasonable?

- What sort of feedback have I sought from students recently? (chats, questionnaires)

Help yourself to appraisal?

- Have I examples to hand of how I changed my approach on the basis of feedback from students?

- Have I discussed teaching/learning matters with colleagues recently? Did I change anything based on such discussions?

- Who seems to be the best teacher that I know? Why is this so?

- Who seems to be the worst teacher that I know? How am I better?

Obviously, this is a checklist for private use! Equally obviously, it is far from complete. However, with the exception of the last two questions, it could be used as an agenda for informal discussion with close trusted colleagues. Individuals' answers to various questions could be compared. More relevant questions could be added, irrelevant ones deleted. Such a checklist could even be discussed (in part at least) with selected students. It may be possible to discuss it with a head of department - who may be able to furnish some additional questions - which could be pointers towards real appraisal issues to come!

The sort of checklist above may look nothing like the criteria by which formal appraisal may proceed. In fact, the sort of checklist I'm suggesting will be a good deal more demanding and penetrating than any general appraisal device. I would suggest that an honest personal checklist should embrace everything that is likely to be involved in formal appraising of teaching performance. If you can live with your personal checklist, you should expect to survive appraisal with flying colours!

Conclusions

Being appraised is not to be feared if we're already well practised at checking - objectively - that we live up to a rigorous set of performance criteria. Appraisal is just an extension of something that has always been with us. In fact, moving appraisal towards the centre of the jobs we do is likely to be fairer to us than previous appraisal methods which tended to assess peripheral activities we did. How often has a teacher been promoted because of *research* evidence, rather than evidence of effective teaching? If appraisal of teaching performance can be done objectively, it will help those whose best work is done behind closed classroom doors. But far more important, if we can develop a climate where we are all *seeking* appraisal evidence about our work and self-appraising our teaching, the learning experiences of our students will be enhanced.

About the author

Phil Race is Professor of Educational Development at the University of Glamorgan. He was trained a long time ago as a scientist, but became progressively more interested in teaching and learning - learning in particular. He believes in active learning - whether in lecture-rooms, tutorials, individualised studying - or in conference audiences! Most of his recent publications focus on active learning in one way or another, including:

The Open Learning Handbook (1989) Kogan Page, London.
53 Interesting Ways to Write Open Learning Materials (1992) TES, Bristol.
500 Tips for Students (1992) Blackwell, Oxford.
A Fresh Look at Learning (1993) Training and Development.
500 Tips for Tutors (with Sally Brown) (1993) Kogan Page, London.
Producing Teaching Materials (with Henry Ellington) (1993) Kogan Page, London.
The Educational Technology Handbook (with Fred Percival and Henry Ellington) (1993) Kogan Page, London.
Workshops that Work (with Tom Bourner and Viv Martin) (1993) McGraw Hill, Maidenhead.